'Rosie Miller has drawn on her many years of practical experience to create a fresh and readable guide to finding one's own leadership style. It is essential reading for anyone wanting to upgrade their thinking and impact as a leader of people and organisations.'

David Birch, Business Director, Ashridge Business School

'Are you a Badger or a Doormat? shines a powerful light on to the dilemmas leaders struggle with and shows you how to develop as a better leader. Any reader will gain a great deal, to the benefit of themselves and their organisations.'

Professor Clive Morton, OBE, Middlesex University Business School

'Until I read this book I never saw the dynamic nature of leadership so clearly. The five dilemmas and the Inner Compass form a unique and compelling way of understanding my own leadership in a practical and useful framework.'

Ian Helps, Partner, KSS Consulting

'Rosie Miller offers practical, non-academic advice with a sound research base amongst leaders. The style is friendly but structured. This is an excellent book for anyone being promoted into management or leadership but would also be a great "health check" for experienced people.'

Eric Pillinger, Director, TACK International Training

'There are numerous books on leadership but few that are as engaging, straightforward and practical as this. Written by one of the country's leading executive coaches, the Badger or a Doormat is not simply a description of good leadership practices, but a practical guide to becoming a good leader.'

Alistair Schofield, MD, Extensor Ltd

Are you a Badger or a Doormat?

FT Prentice Hall
FINANCIAL TIMES

In an increasingly competitive world, we believe it's quality of thinking that gives you the edge – an idea that opens new doors, a technique that solves a problem, or an insight that simply makes sense of it all. The more you know, the smarter and faster you can go.

That's why we work with the best minds in business and finance to bring cutting-edge thinking and best learning practice to a global market.

Under a range of leading imprints, including *Financial Times Prentice Hall*, we create world-class print publications and electronic products bringing our readers knowledge, skills and understanding, which can be applied whether studying or at work.

To find out more about Pearson Education publications, or tell us about the books you'd like to find, you can visit us at **www.pearsoned.co.uk**

PEARSON

Are you a Badger or a Doormat?

How to be a leader who gets results

Rosie Miller

**Financial Times
Prentice Hall
is an imprint of**

Harlow, England • London • New York • Boston • San Francisco • Toronto
Sydney • Tokyo • Singapore • Hong Kong • Seoul • Taipei • New Delhi
Cape Town • Madrid • Mexico City • Amsterdam • Munich • Paris • Milan

PEARSON EDUCATION LIMITED

Edinburgh Gate
Harlow CM20 2JE
Tel: +44 (0)1279 623623
Fax: +44 (0)1279 431059
Website: www.pearsoned.co.uk

First published in Great Britain in 2009

ISBN: 978-0-273-72449-0

British Library Cataloguing-in-Publication Data
A catalogue record for this book is available from the British Library

Library of Congress Cataloging-in-Publication Data
A catalog record for this book is available from the Library of Congress

The publishers would like to thank The Strategic Coach for permission to use material for the figure on page 27, inspired by Dan Sullivan's Weekly Planner™, which is a trademark, copyright, and concept owned by The Strategic Coach.™

10 9 8 7 6 5 4 3 2 1
13 12 11 10 09

Illustrations originated
Typeset in Din 9/13pt by
Printed and bound in Gr

The publisher's policy is
forests.

··

*To all my clients and everyone who simply
wants to do the job of leadership well.*

··

Contents

About the author x
Acknowledgements xi
Foreword xiii

1 Introduction 1
2 The accessibility dilemma 11
3 The communication dilemma 37
4 The flexibility dilemma 65
5 The delegation dilemma 97
6 The change dilemma 127
7 The leadership jigsaw 161
8 The Inner Compass 187
9 Putting it all together 195

Biographies of the Leaders 205
Index 215

About the author

Rosie Miller is a sought-after international executive coach. One of her key coaching talents is to translate complex or theoretical ideas into simple, practical actions busy people can implement.

She has 20 years' experience advising and coaching senior executives on strategy, change, team development, communication and time management. Her clients include leaders in organisations such as Shell, Rolls-Royce, ESB, Water UK, Terra Firma Capital Partners and Deloittes.

Prior to setting up RosyFutures, a company focused on helping people be successful, she held senior roles in the consulting arms of Ernst & Young, Roland Berger and Partners, and Coopers & Lybrand. Her earlier working life in Shell and Conoco gave her direct experience of line management in major corporations.

Rosie is a highly regarded presenter on topics relating to leadership, transition, personal impact and influencing. She brings a deep understanding of how mindsets affect the decisions we make and the outcomes we get. By re-framing old thinking habits into practical new behaviours, she brings positive change. Her experience of supporting people to successfully navigate the dilemmas found in leadership roles led to her sharing her insights through this book.

Acknowledgements

Any enterprise such as a book like this naturally involves contributions, advice and support from many people. I would like to start with a particular acknowledgement of Chico Kidd who originated all the cartoons, added enormously to the creativity and readability of the book and made it fun on the way. I am also enormously grateful to the 20 leaders who gave their time, experience and support so willingly and hope the result does justice to their wisdom.

A huge thank you goes to my hard working band of reviewers who gave such insightful and creative feedback throughout the process. They are Ian Helps, Deidre McEntee, Bob Mason, Michael Cahill, David Deadman, Nicholas Tarrant, Claudia von der Linden, Pamela Taylor, Dorothy Nesbit, Phil Shovlin, Michael McNicholas, Winifred O'Hanrahan, Gordon Balmer, John Campion and Steve Hacking. A big thanks to Liz Gooster, my editor at Pearson Education, for all her excellent advice, suggestions and continual encouragement. A great big thank you also goes to Eddie Obeng for his kind Foreword and to all the people who reviewed the final book and gave such wonderful praise.

I am also indebted to the people who so ably coached me to believe in and deliver this endeavour: Kate Burton, Mahnaz Bhatti, Lynne Fairchild and Margaret Axon. Thank you also to my assistants, Sue Beaumont and Sarah Seabrook, who contributed so much personal support alongside their skills in producing and managing documents – and me! Thank you also to all in the Pearson team, including Martina O'Sullivan, Emma Devlin, Sarah Arnold, Lucy Chantler and Anna Campling, who steered this rooky author so professionally through the process.

But the biggest thank you of all goes to my husband, Eddie Maguire, who spent many days and dinners brainstorming ideas,

ACKNOWLEDGEMENTS

gave encouraging feedback throughout and simply maintained unwavering confidence in both me and 'the book'.

Thank you all.

Foreword

by Professor Eddie Obeng, Pentacle, The Virtual Business School

If, like me, you're suspicious – you shouldn't be. I know that books which promise you 'how to win' or 'how to make it big' sound unrealistic, formulaic and often disappoint, **but this one doesn't**.

Rosie Miller has managed to combine her intense understanding of the transition from good manager to excellent leader with humour and structure to give us a very accessible, memorable and readable book. It is written both as a reminder to you of the 'good answers you've forgotten' and an introduction to you if you're new to the challenges of leadership. Each chapter addresses a challenge you will have experienced yourself. Ever had a decision dilemma? Ever wondered which of your team to spend the most time with? Ever struggled with delegation? And each chapter proposes a way to think about the challenge and practical ideas and solutions developed from Rosie's experience in top-level coaching. She has spiced up the mix with inputs and interviews from real-life leaders from across industry, public sector and surprisingly the military. This means that far from being formulaic, the ideas are well grounded in reality.

So read this gem and discover practical, intelligent and surprisingly effective ways to be a better leader.

Chapter **1**

Introduction

- Leadership – art or science? (p. 2)
- Sleepwalking up the stairs (p. 3)
- Changing mindsets (p. 4)
- Why read this book? (p. 5)
- How to use this book (p. 7)

Leadership – art or science?

This leadership thing is difficult. People want certainty from me but I face so much uncertainty myself!

Leadership often comes with more, not less, uncertainty and ambiguity. Dilemmas are a feature of the job.

At the same time the spotlight on your actions is much greater. The consequences of your decisions are much bigger. How you resolve dilemmas becomes critical – not just to your success but to the organisation's. Making consistently good choices is vital.

From the thousands of hours I have spent coaching senior executives, I have had a first hand view of the dilemmas leaders face and

the most effective ways of resolving them. Less experienced leaders often hold an expectation that there must be a right way – a right answer – and when they know it they will be a good leader!

But effective leadership is a much more dynamic thing. There is no single right point. It's more of an art than a science. Like a tightrope walker you are constantly flexing your behaviours to maintain balance as you make your way forward. In the words of one director, *'It's not black and white. There is a continuum of choices between two extremes. You can't do all the bits well at the same time.'*

A leader's art is choosing the right balance between many, frequently conflicting, priorities. The aim is to make good choices that consistently take forward your team or organisation's purpose and goals. This requires:

> ➤ clarity of direction;
> ➤ the ability to read your current context well;
> ➤ the ability to flex your style to match the context;
> ➤ an ability to take people with you.

This book explores five of the most common leadership dilemmas. They seem to be timeless and universal.

1 What is the best use of my time?

2 How can I communicate more effectively?

3 How do I interact with people to get the best from them?

4 How do I choose, delegate to and motivate people well?

5 What changes will make us more successful?

Because the right choices depend on your individual context, this book will not give you definitive answers. It will give you practical models and tools to create the right foundation for making the right leadership decisions.

Becoming a Proactive Leader will help you focus your time on the right priorities and people. Developing the skills of a Connecting Leader will enable you to manage your communication style and get your message over. Understanding how to be an Inspiring Leader will help you treat people in ways that create trust and motivation. The Coaching Leader knows how to choose people and engage their skills effectively while the Driving Leader decides wisely the changes needed to deliver the group's purpose.

Sleepwalking up the stairs

Many people sleepwalk into leadership roles and don't realise what it really implies. Leadership is not simply a bigger, better (and better-paid) version of what you were doing before, but a different animal altogether.

There are many definitions of the words 'manager' and 'leader' and the activities associated with them. In this book they are defined as follows:

> Leader – the person who sets the agenda and decides the right things to do.

> Manager – the person who does things right to deliver the agenda.

When you are the leader, the agenda-setter, a number of things happen. *Higher visibility is unavoidable*. You have to 'put your head above the parapet' and be accountable for decisions that you think are right for the group. Your words and actions are closely watched. You feel like public property – and in many ways your words and deeds need to be. Consciously or unconsciously you cannot avoid communicating – so better to get a conscious grip on this and send the messages you want to be heard.

Competing expectations are the norm. The number and diversity of people who are stakeholders in your activities is much greater and many will think their needs should be top of your agenda.

You have to stop doing and start being. Most of the actions that deliver the results will be done by others. Your job is to pick the right people, energise them around clear goals and maintain their clarity of direction.

The caterpillar doesn't grow to become a bigger, better caterpillar. He changes into a butterfly because a butterfly has a different job to do. Likewise, a manager has to metamorphose into a leader because the role is significantly different. And just like the caterpillar, you have to make changes if you are to fly.

In the real world of organisations, the difference between leadership and management roles is not nearly as clear cut as change from caterpillar to butterfly. Many people have hybrid leader/manager roles where they set parts of the agenda themselves and manage delivery of a broader agenda. As one leader put it, '**You lead people and manage process**'.

This book is intended to help anyone with a leadership element to their job and encourage them to think about how to develop their strengths as a leader so they can lead higher performance in others.

Changing mindsets

Human beings are creatures of habit. How often do you sit in the same place in meetings, conferences or even your living room? We also have mental habits or mindsets that act as useful mental short cuts to sort information quickly. They let us 'sleepwalk' minor decisions that don't need much thought.

But familiar habits and mindsets need to be updated as we develop and change in life. When we are five years old 'avoid talking to strangers as they may be dangerous' is a good mindset. If we then grow up to become a salesperson, this mindset needs to change or we will find it a struggle to go out and meet new customers!

A fundamental premise of this book is that people can develop their ability to lead others through consciously creating a leadership mindset.

When coaching executives, I hear people using common maxims such as 'my results speak for themselves' and 'my door is always open'. Maybe these maxims have helped them to be successful in the past – or maybe they have simply not been a problem.

It can be very revealing to look behind these 'old friends' and see how you are consciously or unconsciously applying this mindset in practice. Is that the most effective way of operating for who you are now? *Is it the mindset of an effective leader?*

This book invites you to consider and possibly upgrade your leadership thinking habits. As with any good software upgrade, you want your 'leadership upgrade package' to help you:

> operate faster;

> handle greater complexity with ease;

> be more user-friendly;

> be more successful without doing a lot more work;

> do new things successfully.

This book will give you practical and direct guidance on how to upgrade and refine your leadership thinking to bring you and your team or organisation greater success. It has ideas and insights that will be useful for established as well as new or aspiring leaders.

Why read this book?

This book is a practical guide for anyone in a leadership role or aspiring to leadership who wishes to refine their approach. It looks at common dilemmas and dynamics that occur between leaders, their followers and other stakeholders. It offers proven,

practical tools and models to help you re-frame your approach and lead successfully in a wide range of contexts.

Ten years of coaching senior managers and leaders has given me the advantage of helping hundreds of very astute people to become more effective and successful as a leader. The idea for this book came from my observation that certain patterns of thinking were repeated many times across a wide range of executives I coach in companies such as Shell, Rolls-Royce, ESB, Morgan Stanley, Deloittes, BP and AIB as well as a number of charities. Some thinking patterns were clearly more effective than others. My purpose is to share with you my insights on common leadership pitfalls and proven, more effective ways of thinking.

The tools, models and thinking presented in Chapters 2 to 6 are those I use regularly with coaching clients. They have helped many people upgrade and refine their leadership thinking, creating a very positive impact on the team or organisation they lead.

In addition to my own insights for this book from executive coaching, I had the privilege of interviewing twenty highly experienced leaders who are acknowledged as very successful in their own organisations. A short biography for these contributors, collectively referred to in this book as the Group of Leaders, can be found at the back of the book.

They are not necessarily the high-profile leaders who are household names. Instead they are people who are practising the art of leadership every day. They kindly shared their experiences and insights as they recognise the value of creating a practical 'how-to' guide to enable others to learn faster and avoid common traps. As one of the Group of Leaders said, '**any maxim applied without thought is inherently inappropriate because leadership is situation based.**'

Chapters 2 to 6 are the 'how-to' chapters looking at the five most common leadership dilemmas, common traps people encounter around them and ways of steering successfully to deliver your goals.

In my interviews with the Group of Leaders we discussed the principles they use to guide their decisions, as well as their views on the five common dilemmas that form the focus of this book. Useful quotes from these interviews can be found throughout these chapters.

There was such strong agreement between them about how they approached leadership that their common principles are captured in a separate chapter, Chapter 7 – The leadership jigsaw. In Chapter 8, I show how these common principles come together to form a powerful internal guidance mechanism I have called the Inner Compass. The Inner Compass forms the foundation that enables good decision making and sustainable good leadership. It looks at what happens if one aspect of the Inner Compass is weaker or missing and how you can assess your own Inner Compass.

Chapter 9 pulls together the messages from all the chapters. It demonstrates how to think about the interaction of your leadership choices across the five dilemmas and diagnose where changes may make you a better leader. Finally it shows how the strong foundations in the Inner Compass are translated into better daily decisions and better leadership.

As this book was being written, the chapters were reviewed by some experienced leaders and by a number of successful managers who have been newly appointed to broader leadership roles. Interestingly many have commented that the book covers 'really useful practical stuff I've never seen elsewhere'. A number also told me they had shared some of the models with people whose performance they wanted to improve. So the material in this book can also be a useful tool to make it easier to raise issues about behaviours with others.

All the stories and case studies used in this book come from my own experience of coaching and working with people or from the Group of Leaders' own experiences. Names have been changed to protect people's identities.

How to use this book

The book is designed to make it easy for you to go quickly to the ideas that are of most use to you. Some readers may want to start at the beginning and read on but it is expected that many will want to go  immediately to the sections offering relevant help on the leadership dilemmas they face right now.

There are five chapters focusing on the most common leadership dilemmas and the ways you can be a more successful and better leader – a leader who gets results.

Chapter 2 – The accessibility dilemma – looks at issues around being accessible, how best to focus your time and shows how to become a Proactive Leader.

Chapter 3 – The communication dilemma – covers issues around effective communication and shows how to develop skills as a Connecting Leader.

Chapter 4 – The flexibility dilemma – looks at how best to interact with people to become an Inspiring Leader.

Chapter 5 – The delegation dilemma – examines issues around choosing, delegating to and motivating people by being a Coaching Leader.

Chapter 6 – The change dilemma – covers how best to decide whether and when to make changes by being an effective Driving Leader.

Each of these chapters contains the following clearly signposted sections:

➤ *Highlights* containing the key ideas in brief to enable you to scan quickly the content.

➤ A *description of the dilemma* using cartoon caricatures to illustrate two extreme types of leadership behaviour and illustrate the unintended consequences of these extremes in practice.

➤ A *diagnostic* for those who want to assess where they tend to fit between the two ends of the continuum.

➤ *'Balancing wisely'* introduces the leadership mindset that is more effective and the attributes of a leader who successfully manages this dilemma.

➤ The *'how to'* section gives detailed practical thinking, models and tools to let you be more effective at managing this dilemma.

➤ *'In action'* is a case study illustrating one leader putting these tools and techniques into action.

➤ A *summary* of the key points in the chapter.

➤ A list of powerful *coaching questions* designed to help you apply the thinking to your own leadership context and build your own effective leadership mindset.

Some people may want to read the highlights and then try the diagnostic to decide if a chapter is relevant to them. Others may already know they have issues around a particular dilemma and want to go straight to the how to sections. Wherever possible this is facilitated by making each chapter self-contained and self-explanatory.

The purpose of the diagnostic in Chapters 2 to 6 is to help you recognise when you are getting a consistent pattern of results that indicate you may be overusing one set of leadership behaviours. Where you do not experience either of these patterns of outcome regularly you are probably already flexing your choice of behaviour well to meet different contexts and leadership challenges. If you do recognise the pattern of results for yourself, then this chapter will be of especial value to you. The diagnostics will help you focus on which chapters may be most relevant for you to focus on to become a better leader.

Chapter 7 – The leadership jigsaw – and Chapter 8 – The Inner Compass – cover leadership principles that form a foundation to guide you:

> Vision, passion and ambition.
> Values and connecting with people.
> Personal enablers: self-management and self-reliance.

Finally, Chapter 9 – Putting it all together – shows how all the pieces link together to form a powerful model of effective leadership. It then guides you through how to build your capabilities so you have leadership habits that get results.

In developing the characters that appear in this book I wanted to remain gender neutral as, I in my experience, either gender can show the characteristic patterns of behaviour described. At the same time I wanted to avoid gender stereotypes. To meet these aims, Chapters 2, 3 and 4 simply refer throughout to the leader as 'he' and Chapters 5 and 6 simply refer to the leader as 'she'. Any other implication in the use of he or she is unintended.

The fact that you are reading this introduction says that you have an enquiring mind and a desire to know more about the challenge of becoming a better leader.

I invite you to get more curious yet.

By doing so you will learn new ways of analysing what type of leadership is needed in a range of different situations. You will also consciously engage better with people to get improved results.

Finally you will be able to increase your ability to learn and evolve faster yourself and develop others around you to give you and your organisation a competitive edge.

Chapter **2**

The accessibility dilemma – 'My door is always open'

- Highlights (p. 12)
- Accessibility – the two extremes (p. 12)
- Where do you tend to be? (p. 16)
- Balancing wisely (p. 18)
- The Proactive Leader (p. 20)
- The Proactive Leader in action (p. 32)
- Summary of key points (p. 33)
- Coaching questions (p. 34)

Highlights

> Your time is a precious and finite resource for you and the organisation. In this chapter you will learn how to prioritise your time and focus, giving clarity, confidence and momentum to your organisation.

> Doormat Bosses intend to be highly accessible to all but end up spiralling into overworking on short-term, poorly targeted activities. At the other extreme, Badger Bosses are intensely focused on a very narrow strategic agenda leaving no time for many other stakeholders and causing disconnects and demotivation.

> Proactive Leaders prioritise their time and focus by being very clear about their organisation's purpose and vision. This allows them to filter out or delegate some activities and focus on the right people and tasks to attain their goals.

> Effective leaders understand the dynamic nature of leading people and adjust who they are spending time with to fit the context and what they need to achieve. In this way they send a message to others about what is important for the organisation to focus on and they create vital thinking time for themselves.

DILEMMA

Accessibility – the two extremes

As a leader, managing people's access to you and your time is a constant balancing act.

Sitting with a newly promoted leader of a new office in a major consultancy, I heard him complain to a very senior partner: 'I feel very dissatisfied all the time as I just can't see all the people who want and need my time.' The older and more experienced boss replied: 'You'll have to stop worrying about that. Your job is to focus on the most important things to be achieved. To thrive as a leader you have to decide the right agenda and focus on that. Otherwise you'll wear yourself out and still never satisfy all the demands on you.'

THE DOORMAT BOSS

THE BADGER BOSS

At one extreme, the 'Doormat Boss' is constantly available to whoever needs his time and opinion; at the other, the 'Badger Boss' is rarely seen except at dawn and dusk and is always busy on something remote but important.

Both are driven by good intentions but are letting their behaviours prevent them from being effective leaders.

The Doormat Boss's dilemma

The Doormat Boss sees the need for the leader to be accessible in order to listen to people and know what's going on. He wants to make sure that everyone who works for him feels able to call upon his advice and help any time. After all, they need to be getting on with their jobs, and he needs to be supporting them when they need him. Most of all, he doesn't want to be seen as remote, aloof or out of touch. People should be able to come and speak to him about anything at any time. The Doormat Boss is overly focused on helping people with their immediate needs.

But an ever open door invites in guests – both wanted *and* unwanted! Unlike real burglars, Time Burglars don't intend to 'steal'. But they take up time you need for more important things, so that your time feels 'stolen'. One of my coaching clients described it as: '*It starts with an hour or two, then you feel you've lost the week, then the month and so on until you start to wonder where your life is going.*'

Unfortunately, the Doormat Boss's results are often the opposite of his good intentions. Typically:

1 His day becomes so full and cluttered with other people's issues that he ends up with no thinking time. Without this, his responses become increasingly short-term in focus. Or he finds himself endlessly 'taking things away to think about'. That in turn slows down his actual response speed and removes his ability to see the big picture.

2 He finds his working day extending dramatically into evenings and weekends, leaving him tired and increasingly frustrated.

The Doormat Boss spiral

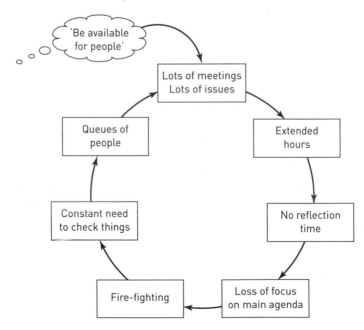

This makes him less open and responsive to things happening round him – new ideas, people's requests and opportunities. He loses the energy and vision to lead.

3 His time is so taken up with anything and everything during the day that those people who should be seen as high priority struggle to get timely discussions or decisions. Important items fail to move forward quickly. He has unintentionally become the block to progress.

4 His employees fail to get the development opportunities that come from solving problems in their own right, leaving a legacy of less capable successors.

The Badger Boss's dilemma

Some Badger Bosses focus on a leader's need to think things through carefully, understand the external environment and develop the big-picture strategy. This requires time to reflect (alone or with a chosen few), check things out with external contacts and develop ideas.

Other Badger Bosses are very focused on the interface between their team and other constituencies and stakeholders. They go to many meetings to promote their team's position and protect their group from unwanted changes driven by other parts of the organisation or externally. It's their way of supporting the group. Overall, the Badger Boss is too focused on the external, longer-term positioning.

THE LOST BADGER BOSS

The unintended consequences of over-focusing on these concerns typically are the following:

1 The leader becomes disconnected from the people he is leading – direction and motivation get lost.

2 He fails to communicate the external knowledge he acquires back to the people he leads, resulting in it failing to influence decisions down the line.

3 Key decisions in his own area get delayed, or people work around him, ultimately risking the delivery of his goals and undermining team morale.

4 He is surprised when his team does things that undermine the careful positioning externally.

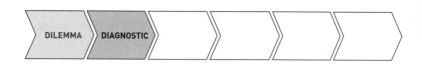

DILEMMA DIAGNOSTIC

Where do you tend to be?

Doormat Boss diagnostic

Read the following and assess if they apply to you. If you consistently agree with four or more of the statements, it's time to rethink who and how you allow access to your time.

1 No time to do 'my thinking' during the day.

2 Endless meetings and chats leading to growing frustration at not being able to get on with 'my things'.

3 Continually extending the working day into evenings and weekends in order to have quiet, focused time.

4 Involved in far more things than you want to be; pulled in many directions all the time.

5 Direct reports and others seem to need more guidance than expected.

6 Always seem to be fighting short-term fires rather than moving the bigger agenda forward.

7 Low sense of achievement despite all that hard work.

Badger Boss diagnostic

Read the following and assess if they apply to you. If you consistently agree with four or more of the statements, it's time to rethink how you are interacting with people.

1 Frustration that your people seem to keep making decisions that miss the bigger picture.

2 Regularly surprised at the things your people go off and do that you didn't know about.

3 Huge amount of email traffic, often from people sitting close to you.

4 Most of your time spent preparing for and managing formal meetings.

5 Regularly leaving or missing internal team meetings for other appointments, for which your team don't seem to understand the importance.

6 Only meeting your own team in formal meeting settings.

7 Team satisfaction and morale lower than you expected.

This chapter explores how to get the accessibility balance right by developing the habits of a Proactive Leader.

Balancing wisely

Time is your own resource and they are not making any more of it so you've got to use it as best you can.

Your time is your most finite, precious and irreplaceable resource. When you are a leader, what you focus on affects not just how your time is spent but also the way many other people following you spend their time. You need to focus that time wisely. When you do so your day becomes more satisfying, your message is clearer, and your follower's actions become more aligned.

Doormat Bosses, who are habitually too easily accessible, tend to be living habits that were successful for them in the past – when they were managers. In some managerial roles it can be important to be constantly available: to give guidance to less experienced staff, make quick decisions, or resolve resourcing issues. Also, most people, including leaders and managers, like to be part of a community and to be connected to people.

Time Burglars walk in because they value time with you on their agenda. Access to the leader or influential person is very important to them. So they make the most of that open door!

But think: Is the time spent with that person the *most* valuable use of your time? What else could you be doing with it? Is it good use of their time – are they denying themselves the opportunity to think and learn from their own experience?

Only you know what *your* key priorities are.

The Badger Boss, on the other hand, is well aware of Time Burglars, and makes sure that he is not diverted from his agenda by distractions. He is clear about his focus and expects others to operate in the same way, with tightly planned meetings to influence senior stakeholders. By handling external relations he may also see himself as protecting his team from

---

[1] Throughout the text, quotations from the 20 successful leaders contributing to the book are shown in bold italics.

external interference and negative forces so they can focus on their core jobs.

Unfortunately, like having a computer firewall that is too restrictive, operating too rigidly in this mode means the Badger Boss can end up missing important or interesting information. It can't get through to him from his own organisation. Alternatively, the Badger Boss may find too late that he knew some vital information that would have shaped what his group are doing – but failed to communicate its significance to his increasingly disconnected managers. Also, by protecting people too much from organisational or external pressures, they are deprived of the clear 'market' feedback they need to constantly sharpen their performance.

People like to have connection with their leaders and don't want them to be shut away in an ivory tower. Many leaders with Badger Boss tendencies are surprised to find good people who report to them leave their organisation feeling disillusioned or dispirited. Even very motivated and diligent followers will disconnect if they find it too difficult to relate to their leader.

Effective leaders are constantly balancing all the stakeholders' needs. There is no right answer to the dilemma of where to be on the continuum between Doormat Boss and Badger Boss. Accessibility is context specific. Leadership is a dynamic activity. Fully effective leaders develop habits that allow them to flex their accessibility deliberately rather than be buffeted by others' agendas.

As a leader, your role is to decide the right things to do – and get others to make them happen. Your agenda for the whole group or organisation needs to be directly communicated through what you talk about, ask about and focus your time on.

A Proactive Leader thinks: 'My door is always open to the right people at the right time.'

When you operate this way several things happen:

THE PROACTIVE LEADER

> Your clarity gives others confidence.

> People understand what to engage with you about.

> Focus and clarity of direction increase throughout the organisation.

> You have time to reflect before making decisions.

> You have time to be responsive to events without losing direction and momentum.

People will know that you have your door open by the fact that you've engaged with them constructively and regularly. Your door is open because you've left the office and not because you are in it!

Clearly delegation is a connected key skill that will help you avoid getting stuck at either end of the accessibility scale. Effective delegation is covered in detail in Chapter 5.

The Proactive Leader

In this book we are defining 'leader' as the person who sets the agenda for the organisation, group or team. Leaders with clear direction and energy are attractive to follow. How such leaders focus their attention and time is one of the principal ways they underline the vision, goals and values for their organisation. It's no coincidence that many people refer to their diary as their agenda!

The key lies in Proactivity. The Group of Leaders[2] spoke of accessibility being more a case of working out whose doors *they* should be walking through. This is not simply 'management by walking about'. It's much more focused and deliberate. It is deciding what you need to know about or communicate, and how best to achieve that within your organisation's context. Being proactive in choosing the most effective use of your limited and precious time is fundamental to good leadership.

First of all you need to be absolutely clear on what matters and secondly you have to use your time as efficiently as possible.

The three essential parts of proactivity are: prioritising, planning and voting wisely.

[2] The Group of Leaders refers to the 20 successful leaders interviewed for this book whose biographies can be found at the back of the book.

Prioritising

When 'My door is always open to the right people at the right time' becomes your leadership habit, you need to decide *who* is right and *when* is right?

To decide the 'who', start by getting crystal clear about the strategic goals. A very useful question to use when choosing who to spend time with is 'How is this person or issue connected to moving our strategic goals forward?' Many acknowledge with delight how much faster and easier decision making and diary management gets when their strategic priorities are clear – and applied!

PRIORITIES
1. ....
2. ....
3. ....
4. ....
5. ....

You also need to be clear about the following:

1 *Your unique role* – what only you can do for the group/organisation, either because of your position or your individual skills – things you *must* do.

2 *Areas of involvement* – what things others will drive, but you need to play some role in – things you are *involved in*.

3 *Areas of being informed/consulted* – what others lead but need you to know about and possibly consult you on – things you are *told about*.

To illustrate this, imagine you are the CEO of an organisation. You have a *unique role* to play in deciding the need and timing of a strategic change. You may consult others and you may need to persuade board colleagues, but it is your job to decide whether to make a change or not. You may then ask someone to lead a strategic change programme for you. You will want and need *to be involved* in the change programme at specific times if it is to be successful – but you do not need to lead it on a day-to-day basis. The person leading the change may decide who to pull into their team, and may want *to inform or consult with you*, but essentially it is their decision.

These types of questions may not be decided by one individual alone. A team may ask one member to play a leading role on some task. Ideally, the team as a whole will have clarity about what is that leader's unique role, their areas of involvement and areas in which they are informed and/or consulted. It is also important to agree what is in each category for other team members.

One leader spoke of moving from being a manager of a team to a more hybrid leader/manager role of a bigger department. He initially made the mistake of thinking he personally had to make all the departmental management tasks happen, leaving his direct reports to focus only on specialised technical tasks. After a few months he re-evaluated his leadership role and realised it was an inappropriate use of his time and his position. He was still thinking purely as a manager.

He realised his reports could take a share of management. For his direct reports the tasks were often new and stretching but only took a small portion of each person's time. As a result, the leader freed up his time to focus on driving strategy and client delivery, and his reports widened their ability to contribute to the firm and grow as future leaders.

A word of caution – it is easy to fall into the trap of focusing only on the explicit, visible, 12–18-month goals and forget those implicit ones that go with leading people in an organisation. Things such as developing a cadre of capable future leaders within the organisation, and ensuring governance is well executed, are part of your job too. A well-balanced leader is aware of all these wider responsibilities, and typically has clear medium- and long-term objectives for these, alongside the more explicit, core business goals.

Priorities need to and will change over the course of a year or over a cycle of strategic change. Which stakeholders get more of your time, and when, will therefore vary significantly. Effective leadership is a dynamic activity and your position on the continuum between Doormat Boss and Badger Boss will vary by task and context.

Doormat Bosses end up stretching themselves too thin by giving apparently equal weight to a large number of tasks. The resultant reactive mode they end up in can be turned around by being much clearer about what they should prioritise and focus on and learning to say 'not at the moment' or delegate to others. Badger Bosses need to consider whether, in setting their own priorities so tightly, they have become detached from one or more key constituencies. They need to include in their priorities time for listening and learning from all their stakeholders – and making them feel connected with the common agenda.

One of the Group of Leaders described how his time and focus changed as he undertook a major strategic programme. At the start of the process he had to make up his own mind whether to commit his whole organisation to an investment in a construction programme that was far bigger and more complex than anything his company had done before. During this phase he proactively sought the views of a very wide range of stakeholders (including his own team members) and external experts. (For more on deciding whether to make strategic change see Chapter 6.)

Once he was personally committed to going ahead, he needed to get his senior team equally committed to a common goal. This involved frequent and intensive debate amongst his top team – a period when they focused on inward dialogue together rather than outward dialogue with others.

When his top team was fully committed and the direction and message were clear, they needed to bring the other organisational leaders, the group CEO and other directors, on board. Finally, with these stakeholders on board, they turned the focus of their time and effort into communicating the strategic message outwards. Their purpose at this stage was to build belief and confidence throughout the organisation and enlist external and internal stakeholder support.

During this last phase, the leader himself made a priority of being very accessible to all staff, specifically appearing at many communication meetings to reinforce the message and hear staff concerns, comments and hopes. He knew this behaviour effectively underlined the importance of these goals to the organisation.

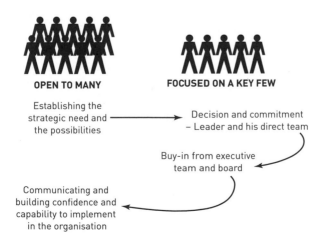

OPEN TO MANY

FOCUSED ON A KEY FEW

Establishing the strategic need and the possibilities ⟶ Decision and commitment – Leader and his direct team

Buy-in from executive team and board

Communicating and building confidence and capability to implement in the organisation

Knowing where you want the organisation to go and what needs to change, makes prioritising the 'who' to spend time with and 'when' much simpler. Your priorities will then become the focus of others' action.

Planning

Prioritisation of necessity involves some filtering of requests for your time and some active engaging with others. A basic plan for your time can help. Yes, we're talking about time management and your diary. Who controls what goes in it? Is it you, your personal assistant (PA) or 'the system'? More importantly, is it managed proactively with a clear set of guiding priorities, or reactively – ending up with a haphazard mixture of things to do?

By now some of you may already be mentally pushing back with thoughts like 'I don't like being over-planned' and 'I need the freedom to respond to people' or even 'I'm at my best when I can be spontaneous'. These may well be true, but if you are to get the best out yourself *and* let others work effectively around you, a degree of planning and process is required.

Ensuring that all your priorities are getting balanced attention will enhance your ability to be flexible, responsive and still driving forward. A little planning ensures your time and talents, and those of others, are focused on the real priorities. If you work best when being spontaneous, can you schedule in and protect some 'open time' to work in whatever ways suits you at that moment?

Whoever makes the actual physical appointments in your diary, you need to be in control of the time allocation. If you have a PA or secretary, they need to understand the priorities, how you work best and how much time to give things. They act as your filter so you also need to work with them to hear what requests come in for your time and help them suggest alternatives, because not all requests may or should be met.

This is not about building a fort with the 'Killer Secretary' seated at the drawbridge. It is to let you focus your time and energy effectively between the three types of activities discussed above: things you uniquely have to do, things you need to be involved in and things you need to be informed and/or consulted on.

One leader told me, '*A sort of mini-test I use is to look at the week or two ahead and assess: how much of my diary am I proactively controlling, seeking meetings etc. versus finding meeting requests from people that require me to be reactive. The more I set the agenda and seek people out, the more effective I am. It also means my diary is 70–80% full so discretionary meetings must be short and focused for the balance of the time*.

Most people and organisations use electronic diaries and automated meeting request systems. Essentially the same rules apply about creating a sensible filter to requests. Choose options that allow you to control what does and does not get accepted in your diary. Make sure others' expectations are managed respectfully – starting with being clear about what time is not available as you already have a use for it. Proactive Leaders understand they need time to do the tasks they have planned and time for catching up and responding to others. They block out parts of their diaries accordingly. If others can see your diary, make sure you have indicated clearly what time slots are actually available and what are not.

One way to 'filter' requests is to accept virtually all meeting requests but significantly limit the time on the less important ones. Unless you are very good at cutting conversations short, this can be dangerous if the discussion is in full flow or unresolved when the allotted time has passed. Some leaders manage that issue by asking for a voicemail or email first so they can judge their answers and/or the time required. One leader I met even took it as far as asking for all requests to be expressed in one 3-minute voicemail or less! This allowed him to respond by voice quickly wherever he was in the world and keep on top of a very large number of tasks. It also made people think hard and get to the point quickly in their communication.

'*You can be a popular leader by being interested in everyone and having time for them but on your own terms.*'

Another practical filter system used by one of the Group of Leaders was a sign on his door saying:

Before you knock on this door:

1 What is the problem you want to see me about?

2 What are the three best possible solutions?

▶

3 Which do you think is the best of those solutions?

4 Go away and do it!

Getting rid of too many requests can be difficult. Clearly prevention is better than cure. One of the most effective systems mentioned regularly is to develop a persona around you that indicates you are actively focused and people need to think carefully about the necessity of contacting you. As one leader put it, *'You need to cultivate an air of being busy and industrious, partly for defensive reasons and partly to set a good example.'*

You will always have requests. Being direct but polite with people is by far the best course. Saying 'I'm really sorry but now is just not convenient. Can we meet later/tomorrow if need be?' often leads to the person coming with a very clear agenda or finding another way to sort their issue. Balanced leaders know they need to make time available for people where it matters – and if they are being Proactive Leaders they will know what matters.

Be alive to the benefits of evolving meeting technologies that increase your communication capability while reducing time, cost and wear and tear on you and others. These include audio conferencing, facilitated audio conferencing, video conferencing and web meetings.

The Badger Boss is very good at planning and structuring his time. His biggest learning is to include some less structured time to listen and engage with others' agendas more openly.

The Doormat Boss finds time planning difficult and needs to connect what he spends time on with the goals and outcomes to be achieved. In this way the Doormat Boss can learn to think forward and proactively use his time to focus on the key priorities.

Principles of good time organisation The time-planning principles devised by Dan Sullivan of 'The Strategic Coach'[3] allow many people to improve their effectiveness. These are summarised in the table opposite. The reason they are so effective is they are built around the key outcomes you want – *not the tasks done but the outcomes achieved.* This subtle but vital change:

> maintains your focus on what needs to happen, keeping everything results-focused;

[3] Sullivan, D. www.strategiccoach.com.

> increases your ingenuity and creativity to find ways to make things happen – maintaining relentless drive towards goals;

> maintains your resilience to setbacks – engaging your strength of purpose and determination.

A Proactive Leader models these positive qualities for others through their own behaviours.

This time-planning system also helps you plan and work with your PA or secretary as they can easily understand the key priorities and how the workload needs to be scheduled.

Time planner

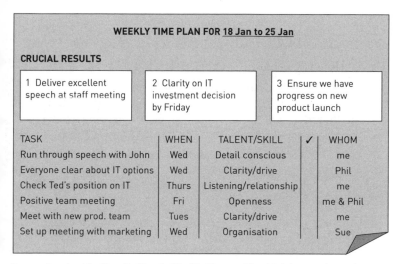

WEEKLY TIME PLAN FOR 18 Jan to 25 Jan

CRUCIAL RESULTS

| 1 Deliver excellent speech at staff meeting | 2 Clarity on IT investment decision by Friday | 3 Ensure we have progress on new product launch |

TASK	WHEN	TALENT/SKILL	✓	WHOM
Run through speech with John	Wed	Detail conscious		me
Everyone clear about IT options	Wed	Clarity/drive		Phil
Check Ted's position on IT	Thurs	Listening/relationship		me
Positive team meeting	Fri	Openness		me & Phil
Meet with new prod. team	Tues	Clarity/drive		me
Set up meeting with marketing	Wed	Organisation		Sue

Source: Inspired by Dan Sullivan's Weekly Planner™, which is a trademark, copyright, and concept owned by The Strategic Coach Inc. All rights reserved. Used with written permission. www.strategiccoach.com

Time Planning principles

These principles are described assuming a weekly planning habit but can easily be adjusted for fortnightly or monthly planning.

Essentials

1 Start with the outcomes you want, rather than tasks you have to do. Write down 3 or 4 crucial results you need to

▶

make happen. Those are your highest priorities for the week and should have appropriate time allotted for them in your diary.

The 'what'

2 Write down the tasks you have to do during the week – some relate to how you intend to deliver the crucial results and others will relate to ongoing tasks you are involved in. Treat your meetings as tasks, remembering to allow some preparation time or follow-up time where necessary.

The 'how'

3 For each task, ask yourself what specific talents, skills or qualities you have that will help you to achieve it. For example, if you have to get two peoples' agreement on a complex project, and you have a talent simplifying complex things, then be prepared to use it! Another person might use their talent to build win–win solutions. Writing down the skills or talents you bring to the task allows you to think through how to be successful. (For more on your unique talents see Chapter 5.)

Delegation

4 For each task in turn ask yourself: *'If not me then whom?'* Who could do the task better, faster, more effectively than you? Who maybe has more time than you? Who would find it more pleasing to do than you? This is a fundamental delegation stage. If someone else is better placed or suited to a task then ask them to do it. In particular, delegate away tasks where you have no specific talent or skill and which do not require your leadership authority or position to get done. You are not the best person to do these! (For more on delegation see Chapter 5.)

Clarity of message

5 Consider your key message or questions for others this week. Many people practise an 'elevator' speech in case they meet you, the leader, in the elevator. You need to know your message or question for your stakeholders too!

Time allocation

6 Finally, look at the tasks that are left. Which day offers the best place to do each task? If there are clearly too many for the time you have, either say 'no' to some, delegate more or roll them over to the next week. If you keep rolling the same task over it's definitely time to review why it's on the list, and probably time to say 'no'!

Many experienced and authentic leaders intuitively apply these principles without the need to write things down. However, if you struggle with time allocation, going through this type of exercise may help you understand where your current processes are not supporting you to be your most effective. You may also want to consider the Inner Compass model described in Chapter 8 to understand where and how you can build your leadership capabilities to manage time more effectively.

Many in the Group of Leaders described how they make sure they are talking to the right people at the right time by connecting the communication process to meetings and gatherings they choose to attend. Their selection of which events to attend or make happen is very directly linked to their purpose and outcomes. These could include formal and informal meetings to hear views and ideas from people as well as meetings to allow them to broadcast their message. Effective leaders recognise there are meetings where simply their presence indicates support and interest in a topic. Your visible interest can be the message you want your followers to see and hear.

The fire-fighting syndrome An element of fire-fighting occurs in any leader's and manager's job. Indeed some leaders are defined by their response to a crisis. But if you find yourself continually putting out fires and you don't get the time to stand back and think before the next one hits you, then it's time to upgrade your leadership habits. Doormat Bosses are far more likely to get into fire-fighting mode than Badger Bosses as they lose focus on the longer-term goals and get sucked into short-term tactical issues.

The work of Roger Bohn[4] suggests the root causes of fire-fighting are:

1 An overloaded system.

2 A culture of tolerating 'fixes'.

3 Poor feedback between linked processes.

4 Relentless deadlines that must be met at all costs.

5 A culture of rewarding fire-fighting behaviour.

As a leader, be aware that successful fire-fighting has a tremendous buzz for the people directly involved. If you have a taste for this buzz yourself you may be part of the problem. In fire-fighting mode you can quickly move from inspirational leader to exasperating manager who is unwittingly supporting the root causes of the fires.

You, and the leadership team around you, can decide whether the root causes of fire-fighting are tackled and reduced or tolerated and possibly rewarded. Your job is to create conditions where sustainable growth and high performance can deliver value to customers. The seductive short-term proactivity of fire-fighting will distract you from making sure your door is open to the right people at the right time to create positive growth conditions.

Voting wisely

Sadly, you can only use any particular hour once. Choosing how to use that hour is like voting – it's an either/or choice. If you choose to see Ms X on a certain project for an hour you are not able to use that hour to think through and prepare for meeting Mr Y.

For some leaders, the hardest lesson is that you really can't please all of the people all of the time. Leaders who fully step into their role attract attention and command respect. People naturally want to pull that leader's focus on to their project – or get the leader's approval of their ideas.

Some leaders find they have a very high desire to meet all requests and apparent needs – this is often a driver in Doormat Bosses. Accepting that you have to be selective is vital if you are to avoid becoming bogged down in low-priority activities. This acceptance is

---

[4] Bohn, R. (2000) 'Stop Fighting Fires', *Harvard Business Review*, July–August.

also vital to avoid overload and fatigue. You also have to let go of the need to be liked and replace it with the desire to be respected.

Sometimes the person you want to please is yourself. Maybe you enjoy discussions with a wide range of people and find yourself prioritising aspects of your job that facilitate this activity. Or maybe you get very enthusiastic about particular ideas and want to be wholly absorbed in driving those at the expense of other aspects of your role.

To be accessible to the right people at the right time leaders have to constantly balance their desire to please themselves or please others with the strategic needs of the organisation as a whole. Successful leaders constantly consider what the group as a whole needs. The art of reading and leading a group is covered in more detail in Chapter 4.

> The leader of a large charity told me how she was constantly balancing her external commitments with the need to drive a major reorganisation. She personally enjoyed taking part in national forums where policy for her sector was created. However, she was very committed to the goals of the reorganisation and therefore was willing to give significant time and focus to personally less satisfying tasks, ensuring the detail was worked through fairly.

Acknowledging your own needs and preferences is very important. Having an open door to the right people at the right time can call for some tough choices. Doormat Bosses may find that creating physical time and space between when they receive a request for some time and when they agree to it in the diary helps them filter more effectively. Badger Bosses need to be alive to the full range of needs amongst their stakeholders and engage more meaningfully with their followers.

Trusted leaders make sure that how they vote with their time and energy matches what they say is important and valued round here.

The Proactive Leader in action

Developing into a Proactive Leader is illustrated by the story of Anne. Anne was the CEO of a hospital. As a natural hard worker, the huge workload and long hours didn't seem a problem at first. But slowly, occasional weekend working spread to every weekend. She found herself going to work earlier every day to give herself thinking time. She sought coaching support when she recognised that she was getting too tired to respond at her best, or even flexibly, and the strategic long-term thinking was not getting done.

The coaching started by looking at what was in her diary every week – and why. The diary was being filled, with no clear filter process, by her PA. Anne's first proactive action was to set her own clear priorities for her time, connected to her strategic goals for the year. She then designed some simple, priority-based time management principles and agreed these with her PA.

One major change was to start by identifying what outcomes she uniquely needed to deliver herself, that week, month and quarter. This was then translated into specific time slots in her diary when she focused purely on them. Including time during the working day for thinking and reflection was new to Anne – and very welcome!

A second significant change was to make only certain times of the week available for people to book appointments on an ad hoc basis. This allowed her to be open and responsive to a wide range of issues in a short time-frame. To ensure she was always in touch with major events, her PA and staff had standing instructions about what sort of high-priority information she was always to be interrupted to hear.

One result was that she found her PA was excellent at managing a queue of requests into the smaller time space. Also, a number of people, when faced with the need to book a specific time, decided they could do without the meeting and went on to resolve their issues successfully themselves. The third result was that people came to Anne better briefed because of their specific (and shorter) time slots.

Within weeks Anne was focusing her time effectively on the strategic priorities for the organisation. She now had the energy to drive projects proactively, inviting people in at the right time or going to talk to them in their own environment. Some months later the board, with the major shareholder, proposed a merger with another hospital. Anne found she now had enough time, space and energy to embrace this strategic move and show effective leadership in the process.

| DILEMMA | DIAGNOSTIC | LEADERSHIP UPGRADE | HOW TO | IN ACTION | SUMMARY |

SUMMARY OF KEY POINTS

1 As a leader, managing access to you and your time is a constant balancing act between two forces: being available to stakeholders and driving your own agenda.

2 The leadership habit that supports a Proactive Leader is *'My door is always open to the right people at the right time'*.

3 The keys to being proactive are: prioritise, plan, and vote wisely.

4 Leaders underline the vision, goals and values of their organisation through what they focus their attention and time on.

5 To decide who are the *right people*, start by being crystal clear about the strategic goals.

6 Your people and time priorities are likely to change as you move through cycles of strategic thinking and implementation.

7 To be with the *'right people at the right time'* involves active linking of your time and diary management to the priorities. The most effective time planning is results focused – not task based.

8 Leaders need to recognise if they are unwittingly supporting a fire-fighting culture. Proactively creating the

▶

conditions where sustainable growth and high performance can deliver value to customers is rarely achieved
when fire-fighting.

9 To be accessible to the *'right people at the right time'*
choices need to be made with the wider needs of the whole
group or organisation in mind.

10 When you become a Proactive Leader you gain vital time to
think and reflect, and the energy and resilience to lead
change. Most importantly, you create an organisation that
is focused on the strategic goals with you.

Coaching questions

How to focus your time and energy most effectively is a perennial
question for leaders. This section contains powerful self-coaching
questions to consider.

To get the most benefit from using these questions, ideally follow
this process:

1 Book out some time in your diary for uninterrupted thinking
and reflection.

2 Find a place where you find it easier to think – this may be a
quiet meeting room, somewhere at home, a favourite walk or a
café or restaurant. Learn where you think best.

3 Take time to consider the questions carefully and honestly
taking account of any feedback you are getting – intended and
unintended!

4 Ask yourself if there are any patterns in your behaviour over
time and if so whether those patterns are still serving you well
as a leader.

5 Write your answers down, especially your actions and the
time-frame in which you will do them. This will increase the
likelihood you will take action as a result. If you prefer, record
them on a voice recorder so you can listen again to review
later.

6 If you prefer to talk things through, find someone who you trust to talk through the questions and your answers but again write down your resultant actions and the time-frame in which you will do them.

7 Book time in you diary now for reviewing and updating your actions in four to six weeks' time.

Clarity of direction

> *Are the vision, goals and values of the organisation clear to me? If not, what is the next step to get this clarity?*

> *How does this use of my time fit in with the strategic priorities?*

> *What message do others read from my choice of focus?*

> *What message do I intend to send?*

Choosing and delegating

> *What things can I uniquely do in the organisation/group either because of my position or my individual skills and strengths?*

> *What things do I need to be involved in?*

> *What things do I need others to drive – and I only need updates or occasional consultation on?*

> *Am I the best person/right person to do a particular task – who could I delegate to who is better or better placed?*

> *If I don't do that task now (or make that decision now) then when – if at all?*

> *How can I communicate my priorities positively?*

Use of time

> *Am I using an effective filter and time-planning system to organise my time – if not then what options do I have that may be more effective?*

> *How much fire-fighting do I and my top team do?*

> *What causes the fire-fighting?*

> *What does fire-fighting cost us in terms of lost focus, lost opportunities, over-worked staff or poor customer service?*

➤ *Does fire-fighting play to my strengths – and if so how can I turn those strengths to creating stable growth conditions in the organisation?*

Voting wisely

➤ *When do I experience conflict between doing 'the right thing for the group' versus pleasing others – or myself?*

➤ *What value or personal quality can I tap into that will help me balance pleasing others or myself versus doing 'the right thing'?*

Positive change

➤ *How will I know I am becoming a more effective Proactive Leader – what are the signs?*

Chapter **3**

....

The communication dilemma – 'My results speak for themselves'

- Highlights (p. 38)
- Communication– the two extremes (p. 38)
- Where do you tend to be? (p. 44)
- Balancing wisely (p. 45)
- The Connecting Leader (p. 48)
- The Connecting Leader in action (p. 59)
- Summary of key points (p. 61)
- Coaching questions (p. 62)

Highlights

➤ In this chapter you will learn how to flex your communication wisely across a wide variety of stakeholders.

➤ Connecting Leaders know that good communication is a vital part of their task and hold the mindset 'I connect people to the results we produce'.

➤ Misunderstood Martyrs fail to engage effectively with senior and external stakeholders while Empty Trumpeters love to do that at the expense of managing delivery of results. Both need to develop a better balance of communication and delivery skills – they need to learn to manage the message and the result.

➤ Effective leaders attract and build strong followers through their ability to engage them with the organisation's purpose.

➤ Different styles are required for different situations and groups of people. When you can use these styles with ease and authenticity you are perceived as a more effective communicator and leader.

DILEMMA

Communication – the two extremes

Your results might speak for themselves, but are they being heard by the right people in the right way?

Steve, a highly capable leader in an engineering firm, had a strong delivery team reporting to him. He asked for coaching to help him get the promotion that, despite great results, had eluded him for some years. The coach questioned him about how he spent his day, who he talked to and about what. It was clear from the answers that Steve was highly focused on enabling his team to deliver and spent relatively little time communicating with senior decision makers and his peers. When the coach enquired why that was, Steve replied 'Well I only go to them when I have something important to tell them. Besides, my results speak for themselves. I let others do all that political stuff.'

What, when, to whom and how – communication is, like many leadership tasks, a balancing act. At one extreme, the 'Misunderstood Martyr' is so afraid of making empty promises *beforehand* and of sounding boastful *afterwards*, he simply fails to engage effectively with key stakeholders. At the other extreme we have the 'Empty Trumpeter'. He is more than ready to create his own thunder, spinning like mad about what is possible while failing to keep an eye on delivery.

Both need to learn the art of managing the message *and* the result.

When they do, they will enhance their ability to influence people and build others' confidence in their leadership. A balance of communication and delivery skills is required to be a fully effective leader. If you tend towards one end of the communication dilemma, this chapter will help you re-balance your communication skills to give you more effective results.

THE MISUNDERSTOOD MARTYR   THE EMPTY TRUMPETER

The Misunderstood Martyr's dilemma

Typically the Misunderstood Martyr understands the need for communication but lives in fear of being seen to blow his own trumpet. Usually he prides himself on excellent results delivery and on needing very little management oversight. At the same time, he is often operating from a mental model of meritocracy. He has a unconscious belief that someone 'above' is watching out for his great results and will fully understand all the benefits and value he has delivered.

This fear of being seen as an 'Empty Trumpeter' means the Misunderstood Martyr fails to engage properly with stakeholders. He fears setting up expectations or appearing arrogant. Even though he and his team do a fantastic job, many Misunderstood Martyrs will move swiftly on to the next task. They shy away from communicating the results and benefits.

When he does communicate his results, the Misunderstood Martyr typically fails to manage the way in which his message is heard and received. This may be by trusting someone else to speak for him and his team without fully checking the quality of how that person conveys the message. Alternatively he presents the results himself but fails to set them in a context the stakeholder can readily understand.

Either way, key stakeholders end up unable to appreciate fully the value and benefits delivered. In turn, the Misunderstood Martyr and his team fail to get the recognition and enhanced credibility. Sadly they also tend to miss the opportunity for celebrating their achievements. This slowly reduces team performance. Recent studies show the brain responds and lifts performance when receiving positive affirmation.

It is very important that people can communicate their own performance in such a way that it casts the appropriate credit on them.[1]

The Misunderstood Martyr runs the risk that someone else, a Credit Collector (consciously or unconsciously), either takes or is given the credit for the value created. Credit Collectors walk in because they understand the importance of creating the right expectations and showing

[1] Throughout this chapter there are quotations from the 20 successful leaders who contributed to the book.

people the relevance and benefits *for them* from the results being delivered by the Misunderstood Martyr.

Many Misunderstood Martyrs feel deep frustration at seeing people who they perceive as 'too focused on the politics' given senior positions ahead of themselves. But failure to recognise their own lack of proactive engagement is part of their problem.

Interestingly, most of the Group of Leaders[2] viewed anyone saying 'my results speak for themselves' as arrogant, or naive or lazy. They saw them as someone who could not be bothered to communicate their results properly and effectively. So sadly, the Misunderstood Martyr can create a reputation for arrogance which is exactly the opposite of what they wanted.

The Misunderstood Martyr spiral

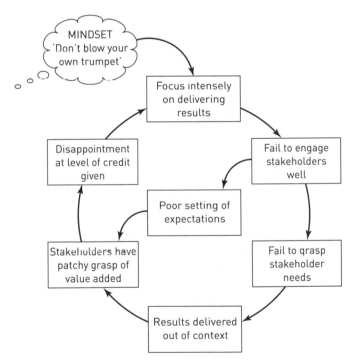

---

[2] The Group of Leaders refers to the 20 successful leaders interviewed for this book whose biographies can be found at the back of the book.

The Empty Trumpeter's dilemma

An Empty Trumpeter wants to please people by delivering on big promises. He spends a lot of time with senior stakeholders and key influencers, taking time to understand their needs, desires and fears. Typically he is a good communicator and a 'big picture' person who is not involved or interested in detail. He is able to paint a very positive and attractive picture of the future that matches stakeholders' and senior leaders' aspirations.

He is often also a risk-taker, able to withstand and even enjoy the tension surrounding significant risk. Often this goes with a cat-like amnesia around previous setbacks or difficulties.

With respect to his delivery team, he wants to motivate them through creating big challenges and opportunities to be the best. He has a strong vision of what could be – and little patience with anything seen as negativity. This can produce exceptional results when all goes well and significant issues, such as large cost over-runs or failure to meet critical deadlines, when it does not.

The unintended consequences of over-focusing on managing the message typically are:

1 The leader makes promises without their delivery team feeling consulted and committed, leading to high and negative levels of tension, risk and fear of failure.

2 The leader fails to listen for or actively discourages negative news from his team, blocking the flow of vital information upwards.

3 Potentially unhealthy competition arises amongst the Empty Trumpeter's peers who perceive him as too political while not always delivering – they reduce their cooperation and support, reducing overall productivity.

4 People start to discount the Empty Trumpeter's projections/goals and become sceptical about their promises.

5 When things go wrong there are damaging hunts to find who is to blame, and overall trust in the leader is eroded.

The Empty Trumpeter's syndrome

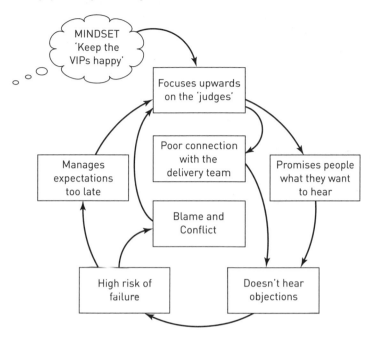

Often an Empty Trumpeter's ability to see and talk about the big picture from a senior perspective means he is seen as a leader of the future. His strong communication skills are rewarded early in his career through a series of rapid job moves. This can lead to a series of jobs where he initiates a big project or change and then moves on before seeing it through to final delivery. As a result, he fails to properly develop the skills or tenacity to lead and manage people through the tougher stages of implementation. If this continues, he starts to get a reputation of leaving a mess behind as others try to pick up projects halfway through.

A balance of communication and delivery skills is required to be a fully effective leader. A useful old saying to remember is: 'The difference between vision and hallucination is implementation'.

DILEMMA > DIAGNOSTIC >

Where do you tend to be?

Misunderstood Martyr diagnostic

....

Read the following and assess if they regularly apply to you. If you agree with four or more of these statements, it's time to rethink how you communicate and to whom.

1 Your promotion path is slower than expected relative to the results you deliver.

2 You are surprised that senior influencers don't seem aware of what you/your team achieve and underestimate your capability.

3 Senior decision makers come to apparently irrational decisions to not back you to lead important, highly visible roles.

4 You are irritated by the many misconceptions and misunderstandings about your area of work/your business.

5 Other people get credit for your/your team's work.

6 You wonder why other people spend so much time on communication.

7 You get feedback that you appear to like doing your own thing and are not necessarily a senior team player.

Empty Trumpeter diagnostic

....

Read the following and assess if they regularly apply to you. If you agree with four or more of these statements, it's time to ask if you are over-focused on managing the message.

1 People start double-guessing or discounting your projections of future results/expected costs.

2 You perceive significant aggressive competition from colleagues – people are less willing to help when the chips are down.

3 Your staff stall and don't seem to engage with the challenge.

4 Staff over-focus on the gap they see between what's possible and what you've promised to others.

5 You often get caught up in unappetising 'blame games' about why things didn't get delivered.

6 You move job regularly and like to have a continual new challenge.

7 You are in danger of becoming very dependent on the goodwill of some key backers and mentors amongst stakeholders.

If you tend towards one end of the communication dilemma, this chapter will help you re-balance to give you more influence and impact.

Balancing wisely

Balancing wisely between managing the message and managing the results is a skill shared by effective leaders.

As shown in the diagram overleaf, Misunderstood Martyrs are good at delivering results (Results ✓) but do not manage the message well (Message **X**). Empty Trumpeters manage the message well (Message ✓) but do not always deliver the results (Results **X**). Those who neither deliver the results nor manage the message well (Results **X**, Message **X**) are unlikely to become leaders. Those that manage both well (Results ✓, Message ✓) become Connecting Leaders.

Good leaders deliver the message and the results

		Low	High
Managing the message	Good	Message ✓ EMPTY TRUMPETER Results ✗	Message ✓ CONNECTING LEADER Results ✓
	Poor	Message ✗ Results ✗	Message ✗ MISUNDERSTOOD MARTYR Results ✓

Managing the results

In general, Misunderstood Martyrs fail to take up fully the leader's responsibility for setting and shaping expectations and messages about their group or enterprise. In some cases they are still thinking like a manager who is delivering objectives set by the leader(s). Now they are the leader themselves, they must build the understanding and buy in to those objectives and the benefits it will produce for the stakeholders. This requires much greater focus on communication and better connection with stakeholders through a different influencing skill set.

> *Leaders have to communicate the results. You need to give emotional commitment and take ownership of everyone's results. They are our results not my results.*

Some Misunderstood Martyrs simply fail to grasp that most stakeholders have very different pressures and ways of seeing the world. As a result, without tailored communication, the delivered results are interpreted in many different ways. Or worse, they may not get noticed at all.

The leader's job is to put the results in meaningful context for the people who need to understand them.

The Empty Trumpeter's overemphasis on managing the message leaves him too little time to focus on leading the delivery team(s). Often he assumes his team is highly capable and that they will find a way of achieving what's required. He fails to recognise that highly capable people still need a leader who motivates and connects with them and the delivery realities. If he encounters resistance from the delivery team, the Empty Trumpeter may be tempted to question if he has the right people for the job. Instead he needs to increase his capability to engage his team and create commitment to goals they can imagine delivering.

> **For both Misunderstood Martyrs and Empty Trumpeters the leadership upgrade needed is 'I connect people to the results we produce'. When you think this way you become a Connecting Leader.**

Connection is fundamental to good leadership. Effective delivery of results requires strong connection in the organisation between actions and the fundamental purpose of the group or enterprise. Cooperation and backing (financial, political, goodwill) comes from connecting external stakeholders

THE CONNECTING LEADER

with the purpose and activities of an enterprise. Managing the message and the results together is a major part of an effective leader's focus.

Being able to connect with peoples' needs and motivations allows a Connecting Leader to:

> understand and shape external expectations;

> express the purpose and objectives of the enterprise in ways that people can accept or find motivating;

> communicate results, positive or negative, in more appropriate ways;

> build trust and cooperation that facilitates better interactions and smoother delivery of results;

> make people feel they are in 'good hands', reducing worry and uncertainty;

> produce a winning blend to inspire others to drive hard on tasks and issues and enabling commitment to high performance (see more on this topic in Chapter 5).

The leader's role in connecting stakeholders

The leader communicates the purpose of the group or organisation and connects the different stakeholders to it

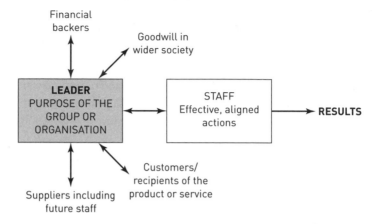

As a communicator I want to give the organisation a sense of where it has come from, where it is going, where we are on the journey and how that is relevant to what you are doing.

DILEMMA   DIAGNOSTIC   LEADERSHIP UPGRADE   HOW TO

The Connecting Leader

'Connecting people to the results we produce' is a vital and sometimes complex leadership task. The messages on this topic from the Group of Leaders are:

1 Take control of the message you want people to hear by understanding and managing your stakeholder expectations.

2 Always make your message consistent but put it in context for the audience.

3 Give credit for positive results to your team and take responsibility for negative news yourself.

4 People are interested in what you've just done and what you intend to do next for them.

Managing stakeholders

The core of good stakeholder management is to understand their interests, needs and view of the world. Leaders vary in their ability to see the world through others' eyes. One practice that is always useful to do, either alone or with the aid of colleagues, is stakeholder mapping.

During the talks dealing with Indian Independence, Gandhi regularly arrived very early for each meeting. While the room was empty, he went round and sat in each participant's empty chair in turn, imagining:

1 What that person's needs were.

2 What pressures they were experiencing from the constituency they represented.

3 What was happening around them.

4 What their hopes and fears were.

In this way he worked out how he could interact with them and communicate his message with each person in ways that met their needs as well as his own.

Stakeholder mapping starts with identifying all the stakeholders that need consideration. There are many ways to do this but one of the most simple and effective is some form of mind-mapping as shown below.

Choose the level of detail most appropriate to your situation. For example, if you are CEO of an enterprise you may work at the level of: customers, the chairman, other board directors, shareholders, your executive team, other senior managers, other staff, unions, key suppliers, etc. If you are the marketing director of a business division then your list might be: core customers, new customers, potential customers, your boss, marketing staff, sales director, other peers, sales staff, key agency contacts and so on.

Key questions to ask yourself in drawing up your stakeholder list are:

➤ Who is vital to my success?

➤ Who is affected by my actions?

➤ Who is interested in my actions?

Stakeholder mapping process

When the list is complete, do the 'Gandhi test' for, ideally each stakeholder, but at minimum key stakeholders, in turn by asking:

> What are their key needs?

> What are they interested in?

> What do they need and expect from me/us?

> What do they hope/fear?

> How do they want to be communicated with – what is their style?

If you are not familiar with doing this, it may seem quite laborious. However, if you keep it simple, honest and to the point, it takes surprisingly little time. The insight gained will be useful on many occasions. If you find you don't readily know the answers to the questions, treat it as a wake-up call.

You will benefit as a leader by taking time to understand your stakeholder needs. Make increasing your understanding an objective in every interaction with your stakeholders. Similarly, use the knowledge of your team and other colleagues to constantly update your picture.

Stakeholder mapping is a particularly useful exercise to do in the first 90 days of a new role or when you are about to initiate any strategic and significant change.[3]

[3] Watkins, M. (2003) *The First 90 Days: Critical Success Strategies for New Leaders at All Levels*, Boston: Harvard Business School Press.

The information from the stakeholder mapping exercise allows you to plan how best to manage the expectations and reactions of key stakeholders. Good communicators realise this is a vital  ingredient for managing the message internally and externally. Misunderstood Martyrs need to focus more on connecting with and influencing the stakeholders who they are expecting to 'judge' their performance. Avoid leaving the understanding of your message to chance.

Empty Trumpeters need to connect more with their delivery team to both motivate the high performance they seek and stay in touch with the delivery reality. They also need to understand the 'optics' of their stakeholders. Investors and city analysts do not like performances that do not meet the expectations set earlier. In general, it is a wise leader who consistently delivers what he has promised – or ideally more. Hence the often used rule: under-promise and over-deliver. Getting that balance right is a key factor in creating credibility and influence.

Know when to communicate

You need to balance the fact that people upwards and externally do not know your results unless you tell them. So you have got to find mechanisms to get them to understand the context and why the result is good and valuable.

Many people have been taught the presentation adage:

> tell them what you are going to tell them;
> tell them;
> tell them what you told them.

Stakeholder management can similarly be summed up as:

> tell them what you are going to do for them *and why*;
> do it;
> tell them you have done it; *and*
> how they have benefited/been affected.

Where there is a vacuum of information, people fill the vacuum. Humans are hardwired to look for negative things in their environment. An information vacuum tends to get filled with negative rumours, fears and cynicism.

In many organisations the 'grapevine' works faster than the internal communications systems. As Douglas Adams[4] points out nothing travels faster than the speed of light except bad news.

For most people, regular updates about what is happening as they go along is better than no information suddenly followed by the fully worked 'answer'. Positive messages need constant reinforcement through a range of ways including:

> management briefings;

> internal newsletters;

> direct emails from leaders;

> interviews with external publications/media;

> informal chats and meetings;

> news posters in prominent places;

> videos featuring senior managers.

In addition to these more 'tell' channels, leaders need to create a number of 'listening' channels. These include:

> Q&A sessions;

> less formal discussions with a cross-section of people inside and outside the organisation through lunches and other social events;

> staff surveys;

> informal walkabouts;

> invitation to email questions and queries direct to the leader (always ensuring they are all answered promptly) or indirectly to allow anonymity;

> interviews with new joiners and with leavers;

> attendance at conferences and other gatherings of interested parties.

[4] Adams, D. (1992) *The Hitchhikers' Guide to the Galaxy*, Heinemann.

Good leaders take a lot of input. They're good listeners. They want not just inputs from their immediate team but also from outside. They'll have a network of people they speak to in order to challenge their own thinking.

A leader who can respond to the issues coming through such channels appears more authentic because they are clearly relating to the stakeholder's agenda. With skill the leader will, through the way they answer the questions or respond to concerns, get their message across.

Different stakeholders will need different communication methods.

How much time to spend communicating with different stakeholders depends on your individual context. As highly successful entrepreneurs such as Richard Branson, Anita Roddick and Mike Ashley have all experienced, leading a publicly quoted company demands significantly different communications with shareholders and city analysts, compared to leading a privately owned company.

Whatever your leadership role, you need to understand fully your stakeholder context and take ownership of the content, style and timing of the message you want them to hear. And if in doubt, remember most leaders under communicate and underestimate the need.

I think in business you can't over communicate. Sometimes we'd say something in one of our bulletins and people would assume that was it – we've told everyone. But you need to say it again – remind people. They won't pick things up or agree with it if it's not said in the right way.

Communicate flexibly

Making a connection with people is a fundamental part of leadership. Many people are familiar with the idea that to achieve anything we have to 'win both hearts and minds'. In his book, *Hostage at the Table*,[5] Professor George Kohlrieser describes the human need for bonding and its role in communication and leadership:

[5] Kohlrieser, G. (2006) *Hostage at the Table*, San Francisco: Jossey-Bass.

'Bonding is that underlying emotional synergy that creates the process for mutual influence. . . . you do not have to like someone to bond with them. Bonding is about an exchange of energy that keeps people engaged in a way that holds relationship together during difficult moments.'

Our communication style is one significant factor affecting how easily we create bonds with people.

One model of communication style which many leaders find useful looks at the 'Blunt Truth' style versus the 'Good Story' style. I am indebted to the very experienced executive coach David Franks for sharing it with me. It looks at how people prefer both to communicate and be communicated with.

People vary in the type of communication they are attracted to and find motivating. Those who prefer to hear the 'Blunt Truth' about things look for facts, ideally stripped of emotion or embellishment. As communicators themselves, they intend to be scrupulously honest. When focused on positive news, they tend towards plain unvarnished facts – usually associated more with left-brain thinking. This type of communicator often leaves the recipient to 'make up their own mind about what that means'.

Positive 'Blunt Truth' communicators connect well with people in situations where, as a trusted source of 'the truth', they offer certainty about information people need to know. This style is less successful

Four types of communication style

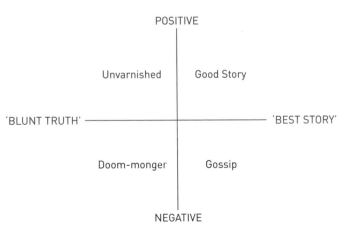

when people need to be uplifted, motivated and connected to positive possibilities. Also, used too narrowly, it can fail to convey the positive emotional context or the benefits for that listener.

A person with a preference for both the 'Blunt Truth' and negative news becomes a 'Doom-monger' in the eyes of others. Their intention may be to warn others of risks and problems. But, their constant pointing out of unarguable negative points results in the undesired effect of recipients closing down and not listening. A good example of this is the person who tries to help someone improve their performance by giving a constant stream of accurate but negative feedback. Eventually their 'help' results in demotivation of the recipient – or the communication simply being blocked out.

At the opposite end of the scale, people who prefer communication to always put things in the most positive light tend to look for the 'Good Story'. They like a well-structured narrative style that engages emotions as well as logic – usually associated with right-brain thinking. Used well, this communication style is very successful for connecting people to positive outcomes and motivating people towards a positive, upbeat state.

Listeners who prefer a 'Good Story' communication style are not necessarily unaware of associated difficulties or risks. They want to be engaged in a way that makes them resourceful and energised. However, used excessively, or seen to be blatantly ignoring negative, unpalatable truths and this style is seen as 'spin'. Prolonged use results in the communicator's words being discounted, or distrusted over time.

In the bottom, right quadrant of the figure we have the people who like information through a story but tend to focus on negative news. Often this takes the form of 'Gossip'. There are many public examples in the relationship between political leaders and the press of how powerful negative stories can be. Good leaders need to be aware of the way in which gossip and rumour forms inside and outside their organisation. Their job is to ensure there is sufficient positive information – facts and stories – to counterbalance this. Importantly, leaders also need to avoid the very human desire to join in gossip. Ideally they want to be aware of it but not join in or be seen to manipulate it overtly.

While most people can do all four communication styles at different times, we all tend to have a preferred style we use most often and are most comfortable with. People who have a strong prefer-ence for 'Blunt Truth' styles alone need to understand that they can be seen as underselling or naive or sometimes rude by people with a strong opposite preference. In change situations, they are seen as unsupportive, negative and not ready to make the change.

People with a strong preference for 'Good Story' styles alone need to recognise that they can equally be seen as naive, manipulat-ing and possibly untrustworthy. Leaders communicating to a group need to ensure they have a suitable message for both styles as both preferences will exist in their audience.

Summary of the four communication styles

Style	Useful for	When overused
Positive 'Blunt Truth'	• Waking people up to realities • Reassuring people that things are under control	• Bluntness seen as rude • Matter-of-factness seen as dry • The complete honesty seen as naive • Seen as unwilling to change or may be a blocker
Negative 'Blunt Truth'	• Acknowledging risks • Surfacing problems	• Doom-monger • Switches people off
Positive 'Good Story'	• Emotionally connecting people to a positive outcome • Creating an upbeat and resourceful state	• Seen as spin • Distrusted over time
Negative 'Good Story'	• Boosting messages about unwanted behaviours and their consequences	• Destructive gossip

Choosing the style to fit the situation and the message you want to impart is very important. Imagine you have a group of salespeople in a room and you want to send them back to their customers full of energy and enthusiasm. In this situation a very positive style, telling a 'Good Story' focused on their achievements, advantages and opportunities is required.

You need to accentuate the positive in every situation, because in the long term people are more motivated in that than they are by threat or fear of bad news.

Alternatively, imagine you are initiating a change programme in response to increasing threats in the marketplace. You need to wake staff up to the reality of the situation and create some urgency of response.[6] This situation calls for communication that helps people see 'Blunt Truth'. But this is unlikely to be just factual: it needs to engage emotions and be seen as true.

Effective leaders learn to flex their style to the situation. Indeed the more someone can move effortlessly and authentically between styles the more likely they are to succeed as a leader. One simple way to improve your own flexibility is to think about who is a good communicator in each style. Imagine how these different good communicators would approach a situation. You can then model their approaches in your communication and watch/listen for the feedback. If it is positive, try some more. If it is negative, flex your style a different way.

> One of the leaders contributing to the book described how he had to flex his communication style between different jobs. When heading up a trading function within the business, the people who worked for him were very focused on the latest news, being up to date and in the know. Their world was fast moving, with competitive edge coming from knowing and using information faster than the next guy. As the leader, he had to make sure his communication was short, clear and direct. Thinking and doing was very much in the moment. In his next job, he was in charge of strategy for businesses with much longer time horizons. His audience was business leaders making decisions with longer time-frames. He had to flex his communication style to be more considered, structured and deliberate.

The real art of effective communication comes from using the different communication styles in certain combinations.

In his book *The Secret Language of Leadership* Stephen Denning looks at how leaders can inspire action.[7] He demonstrates the effect of juxtaposition of a 'Blunt Truth' story showing a negative future followed by a positive, inspiring story relating to the past. This is one of the most

---

[6] Kotter, J. (1995) 'Leading Change: Why Transformation Efforts Fail', *Harvard Business Review*, March–April, pp. 59–67.
[7] Denning, S. (2007) *The Secret Language of Leadership*, San Francisco: Jossey-Bass.

effective ways to get humans engaged with the need to change. It gets you their attention by creating a bond to what you are saying. Then you can use logical and rationale arguments to persuade.

Effective leaders are self-aware about their own communication style and capability. They think through what communication is needed for different situations to achieve the outcome they want. They talk to a range of people to get insight into the group's current focus and emotional climate. If they are not the right person for a communication because they struggle with the appropriate style, they play to team strengths and ask someone to assist. The other person can either help the leader shape the message and style or they might even deliver it for the leader if appropriate in that context. The leader's outcome is always to find ways to connect the audience and the message they want them to hear.

Good communication is a vital leadership skill. Very often your perceived effectiveness as a leader is strongly related to your ability to communicate and connect with people so they become willing followers.[8] Over time, fully effective leaders create an attractive personal leadership 'brand' around themselves, allowing them to recruit and retain highly talented individuals in their organisation.

Take time to get the communication balance right and you will greatly enhance your value and contribution as a leader.

Irene, a manager in a financial services firm, was promoted to a wider leadership role within her division. Her responsibilities now included developing her team and influencing and guiding people who were nominally her peers. While she enjoyed the extra challenge she worried about how her additional efforts would be noticed and rewarded if she was not the one pointing to something tangible and saying 'I delivered that'. Working with her coach, she realised that she was still using old performance measures in her head. In her new leadership role, her success measures included how well she developed talent and how influential she was without stealing other people's thunder. She had to flex her communication style, which was mainly directly 'telling you what I have done/know'. Now she

[8] Reicher, S.D, Haslam, S.A, Platow, M.J. (2007) 'The New Psychology of Leadership', *Scientific American Mind,* August/September 2007.

can choose between that approach and an equally valuable style of shaping ideas through asking good questions, coaching ideas from others and motivating them by promoting their success.

The world out there quite rightly assumes that if a team wins it is also because of their leader. They will see the hand of the leader.

Assigning credit and blame

One of the most common messages from the Group of Leaders is that an effective leader should always give credit for positive results to their team and take responsibility for negative news themselves. While this can seem inherently 'right', many managers who move up to leadership positions worry about how they can still be seen to have delivered any value if it's the delivery teams who get the credit for the results.

The universal message from the Group of Leaders was that effective leaders attract and build strong followers. Ensuring the deliverers get credit for positive news is a sign of strength and integrity in a leader and makes them attractive to work for and with. Similarly, they take responsibility for negative news and the actions required to put things right. In *Good to Great*[9] Jim Collins shows that getting the ego out of the way is a characteristic of Level 5 leadership. In terms of leadership this is a quality that many followers find attractive.

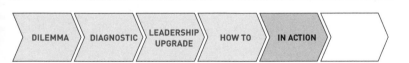

DILEMMA DIAGNOSTIC LEADERSHIP UPGRADE HOW TO IN ACTION

The Connecting Leader in action

Developing into a Connecting Leader is illustrated by the story of Bob. Bob led a specialist team within a large division of an oil company. He had been promoted up through the ranks and was at a job level with leadership responsibilities greater than he had expected.

[9] Collins, J. (2001) *Good to Great*, London: Random House Books.

His highly developed delivery skills in his area, his encyclopaedic knowledge of his customers, his products and his team played a significant role in the competitive edge they had created in the market. But, despite being a major contributor to the bottom line of the division, his divisional boss had little time for Bob.

When Bob first met with his coach, the goals he set were all about driving higher performance so that the team would get more recognition, and thereby more job security, within the division. It quickly became apparent that Bob, in turn, had a low opinion of his divisional boss. He saw him as full of 'spin', unwilling or unable to grasp the importance of Bob's team's contribution to his overall success. The boss's 'high spin' style exemplified everything Bob disliked and distrusted in communication.

The coach asked Bob to look at his own communication style and contrast it with his boss's. When he truly 'looked at his behaviours in the mirror' he realised that honesty was a very strong value giving him a strong need to tell the 'Blunt Truth' at all times, good or bad. Using his own ability to handle 'Blunt Truths', he also acknowledged that this could lead others to sometimes see him as negative or difficult to deal with. He saw that he tended to let 'the numbers' say the positive things about him and his team's performance. In dialogue he focused on the problems, the risks and the things that needed changing. His frustration with his boss's lack of recognition had resulted in him slipping into a style of connecting by focusing on what was difficult, rather than what was good and could be even better.

Shortly after this conversation, the company reorganised moving Bob's area of the business to a new division. Bob was made head of a larger group within Europe and had the task of integrating teams in several countries.

He also changed boss. He took the opportunity to change his communication behaviours and create a much more positive and constructive climate around him. One of the key success measures he set himself was to influence positively how his new boss perceived his communication style.

He decided early in the integration process to run a one-day conference to pull the disparate team together behind the new strategy and goals. He understood that, as the leader, he had a vital role in setting the tone and style at this meeting – and how people worked together afterwards. He also had his new divisional boss watching and listening that day. He wanted her to see him as a leader and not simply a very able technical specialist/manager.

Accepting his own tendency and reputation of focusing too much on the 'Blunt Truth', he consulted with a range of different people as to what the audience needed to hear to motivate them, what the positive messages were and how to put them across in a believable but uplifting way. He also realised that the numbers were not enough. The leader needs to speak from the heart and say where the organisation is going and why.

With this in mind, he developed a very positive but truthful speech. Lastly he practised answering negative-sounding questions with more positive and resourceful responses.

On the day of the conference Bob delivered a resounding and upbeat opening speech, focusing on the joint team's ability to deliver and the opportunities that lay ahead. For the rest of the day and in the weeks afterwards, he was delighted with the way people connected with him and his positive message. He also created an excellent first impression with his new boss.

SUMMARY OF KEY POINTS

1 Communication of the message is a vital part of the leader's job. A leader's ability to communicate is often seen as a measure of their effectiveness.

2 Creating the right balance between managing the message and managing the results is a constant issue requiring focus.

3 The mindset upgrade that supports a Connecting Leader is 'I connect people to the results we produce.'

4 Connection with people, their motivations and their interests is at the heart of successful communication and leadership.

▶

5 The time focused on communication should be significantly higher for a leader. They create the conditions for good results by communicating to managers what needs to be delivered and when.

6 Stakeholder analysis is a valuable and productive method of understanding others' needs and interests. It is particularly useful in the first 90 days of a new role or when launching significant change initiatives.

7 When to communicate depends on your business context and your stakeholder expectations. In general most leaders underutilise the full range of communication channels that exist.

8 Preference about communication style significantly affects how a message is received. Being able to flex communication style is a vital skill.

9 Self-awareness of your own preferred communication style helps you understand your impact on people. It also helps you to know when to flex your own style or use the styles of others to get your intended message across and create the outcome you want.

10 An effective leader manages their ego to give credit for positive results to their team and takes responsibility for negative news themselves.

11 When you become a Connecting Leader you take proactive control of the message you want people to hear and manage the communication process to create that outcome.

Coaching questions

Getting your communication right for your stakeholders is a key part of leadership. This section contains powerful self-coaching questions that will help you think through where and how you can enhance your performance as a Connecting Leader. For more on how to use these self-coaching questions please see the Coaching Questions section in Chapter 2.

Understanding stakeholder needs

> How well do I know the needs and interests of all my stakeholders – including their communication needs and preferences?

> How do I keep that information fresh and up to date?

> How much focus do I give to empathising and reading others' positions? Are there others on my team who are better at this?

> How easy do I find it to articulate the purpose and goals of the organisation to different stakeholders?

> Are any of my stakeholders significantly 'unconnected' right now? If so, what can I do to change that and when?

Communication focus

> How much of my time is focused on communication?

> How do I prepare for communications – do I have a clear outcome in mind, a strategy and action plan?

> Am I using all the communication channels available to me to get a consistent message across?

> Do I have sufficient ways to listen formally and informally to all my stakeholders?

> If I am not achieving the outcomes I want and expect, how might communication issues play a role in that?

Communication style

> What is my natural or preferred communication style – am I more 'Blunt Truth' or 'Good Story'?

> What would others say? Who can give me candid feedback?

> How do I view people with very different styles?

> What benefits do these different styles bring to the organisation?

> For the people I struggle to work with or connect with, how do their styles differ from mine?

> Do I have the same style at work and in my home life?

➤ *How comfortable am I with bonding at an emotional as well as a logical level?*

➤ *How comfortable am I in flexing my style?*

Leadership style

➤ *What personal leadership style will be most effective for me and my organisation?*

➤ *How close is my actual leadership style to my desired or ideal style?*

➤ *What two or three things would make the most difference to achieving my desired leadership brand?*

➤ *How would I know I am becoming a more Connecting Leader? What are the signs of successful change?*

Chapter **4**

The flexibility dilemma – 'Treat others as you wish to be treated'

- Highlights (p. 66)
- Flexibility – the two extremes (p. 66)
- Where do you tend to be? (p. 71)
- Balancing wisely (p. 72)
- The Inspiring Leader (p. 74)
- The Inspiring Leader in action (p. 91)
- Summary of key points (p.93)
- Coaching questions (p. 94)

Highlights

- In this chapter you will learn how to flex your style to influence your followers wisely while still meeting their expectations.

- While Hippie Bosses focus on satisfying individuals' needs, Emperor Bosses focus exclusively on their own views of what the whole group needs. Both constrict their organisations through loss of effective teamwork and undesired conflict.

- An effective mindset for the Inspiring Leader is 'I treat people in ways they perceive as respectful and in the best interests of the group.' Creating strong bonding and ownership of a common cause increases followers' sense of inclusion and being respected.

- What you intend to convey may not be what the recipient perceives. Curiosity is a powerful tool to increase your listening and reading of others.

- Good leaders understand which aspects of the group's culture to uphold and which to change. They are able to read the group's needs and create acceptable, common expectations and boundaries while still treating individuals with respect.

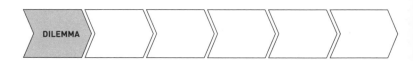

DILEMMA

Flexibility – the two extremes

The words 'fair', 'respectful' and 'open' are often associated with good leadership. They are universal values. But dig a little deeper and one person's view of fairness and openness may differ from another. How do you balance people's expectations?

The owner of an ice cream parlour had three customers waiting for ice cream. It was the end of the day and he only had a limited amount left of three flavours: chocolate, vanilla and toffee. He didn't want to disappoint anyone and he knew from his own experience that all the flavours were delicious. So to be fair, he gave each customer a big dish containing one third of all three remaining flavours. The first customer said 'Oh – I can't eat chocolate. I'm fine with toffee and vanilla'. The second said 'I only really like chocolate – could I have his?' The third customer asked the other two if they would like his toffee and chocolate ice cream as he only came in for a small cone. The ice cream parlour owner went home declaring 'You just can't please these people.'

How you treat people versus how they expect to be treated is an ongoing leadership dilemma.

At the core of this dilemma are two questions:

1 How much should I match people's expectations versus shape them?

2 How do I balance what the group needs versus what the individual wants?

THE HIPPIE BOSS

THE EMPEROR BOSS

The answers to these questions lie along a continuum.

At one extreme, the Hippie Boss wants to meet everybody's individual needs. At the other extreme, the Emperor Boss knows what's best and right for the group and everyone in it.

Both desire to be fair and helpful to people, but their way of being fair can have unintended consequences.

The Hippie Boss's dilemma

The Hippie Boss wants people to be happy and get their individual needs met. He strongly follows the idea that everyone will be motivated and work better if they can make their own choices. Often, he is driven by an underlying desire to be liked and to avoid the negative aspects of conflict. Being overly focused on listening to individuals, he will happily bend rules and boundaries to help someone.

But slowly, the lack of clarity about boundaries and the warm fuzziness about behaviours lead to unintended confusion and conflict. On the surface a lot of 'motherhood and apple pie' statements are encouraged, but in reality the lack of consistency produces uncertainty and slows down decision making.

By being too much 'Mr Nice Guy' the Hippie Boss ends up disappointing and frustrating people. Sometimes people are left with the impression that they had gained support for an idea, only to find someone else's idea is implemented. Frank, an engineering manager, once told me, '*The great thing about Andrew, is that he will always listen to you. The bad thing is he always listens to the next person as well and so he either delays decisions forever or does what the last person he speaks to suggests.*'

The unintended consequences of the Hippie Boss's behaviours are:

1 Conflict is created when people try to implement different 'agreed solutions' in an ambiguous context.

2 By saying 'yes' to a lot of individual terms and conditions, the complexity within the organisation becomes much greater, adding significant cost – or simply becoming unmanageable.

3 People find that the person shouting loudest or asking for most gets most – creating inequalities, frustration and a continual spiral of demands.

4 Managers in the organisation cannot see consistent decisions being made by the leader and so make inconsistent decisions themselves or avoid making decisions altogether.

5 People's development and learning is slowed down as they don't get clear standards set or clear feedback about what is truly expected from them.

Hippie Boss's dilemma

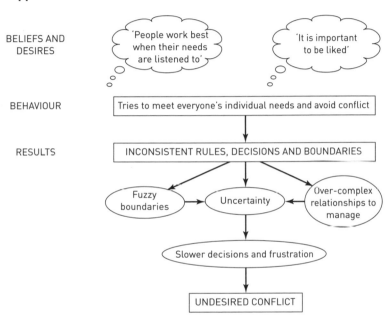

BELIEFS AND DESIRES

'People work best when their needs are listened to'

'It is important to be liked'

BEHAVIOUR

Tries to meet everyone's individual needs and avoid conflict

RESULTS

INCONSISTENT RULES, DECISIONS AND BOUNDARIES

Fuzzy boundaries → Uncertainty ← Over-complex relationships to manage

Slower decisions and frustration

UNDESIRED CONFLICT

The Emperor Boss's dilemma

Emperor Bosses are very sure of right and wrong. They believe they are totally fair because they treat everyone the same. They hold strong values and want these reflected in the behaviours and norms in their organisation. For the Emperor Boss, the needs of the whole group or organisation are their only concern, not the needs of the individual. They know too many differences can lead to confusion and discontent in the group.

Their focus is creating and maintaining clear boundaries and rules. The style of their organisation becomes set by the Emperor Boss's personal norms and behaviours. His or her underlying assumption is 'if it's the right thing for me it will be the right thing for you.' In some cases they become paternalistic, while in others the phrase 'my way or the highway' becomes true.

These types of leaders can be very highly regarded by people who think and behave in the same way as the boss. But this is always a more limited number of people so the benefits of diversity and innovation are lost.

Emperor Bosses appear rigid and inflexible to those who may share the same goals and values but express them in a different way. Too much 'Mr Right Guy' leads to:

1 Organisations ending up with a lot of 'rules' which have to be policed and a climate of fear rather than people understanding the real values and expectations and behaving in line with these.

2 A very black and white approach to what constitutes 'the right way', making it difficult for the Emperor Boss to tolerate alternatives. They then struggle to motivate diverse groups.

3 Disaffection growing in parts of their organisation that are more remote from the leader or where the leader's style is not conducive to getting the best results.

Emperor Boss's dilemma

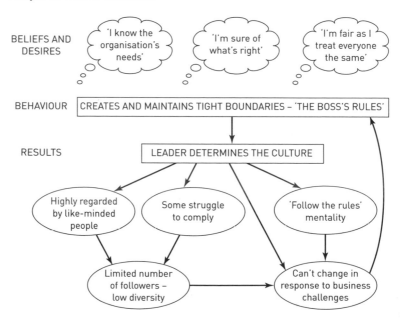

4 The Emperor Boss becoming so much a determinant of the organisation's culture that it is hard for them, or indeed a successor, to lead change when required by subsequent changes in the business environment.

DILEMMA DIAGNOSTIC

Where do you tend to be?

The Hippie Boss diagnostic

Read the following and assess if they regularly apply to you. If you say 'yes' to four or more of these statements, it's time to rethink how accommodating you are being.

1 You regularly have to sort out confusion about what you said and what you meant.

2 You are under constant pressure to make up your mind when you thought it was clear you had.

3 Managers who work for you hesitate to make decisions and constantly want your thoughts/agreements in writing.

4 You have a lot of battles with your HR managers about creating precedents.

5 You struggle to say 'no' to people whose needs differ from the group at large.

6 You get frustrated that members of your team can't seem to resolve conflict for themselves.

7 You are surprised at the level of negativity around you, given you try so hard to keep people happy.

The Emperor Boss diagnostic

••

Read the following and assess if they regularly apply to you. If you say 'yes' to four or more of these statements, it's time to rethink how flexible you are being.

1 You are often disappointed about how many individuals seem to put their needs ahead of the group's.

2 It frustrates you how often you have to adjudicate on behaviours when it should be obvious to people what is right.

3 You struggle to understand people whose heart is in the right place but seem to go about things in strange ways.

4 You experience unexpected conflict with peers about who is doing a good job.

5 People either fit into your team or leave fairly quickly.

6 You are surprised when you hear people consider you were not fair.

7 You seem to encounter a lot of well-intentioned resistance to your style in parts of your organisation.

In this chapter you learn how to flex your style to get the most effective balance between meeting individual needs and setting the tone and style of the group.

DILEMMA   DIAGNOSTIC   **LEADERSHIP UPGRADE**

⚖ Balancing wisely

When you are a leader, your values and how you live by them have a tangible effect on the decisions and relationships in and around your organisation. Like it or not, the leader's words and deeds are watched and analysed constantly.

It is a continual balancing act to influence your followers wisely, while still meeting their expectations.

Both the Hippie Boss and the Emperor Boss have strong values that they are expressing. But one is too focused on meeting the needs of individuals, while the other is too focused on shaping the group's behaviours.

The Group of Leaders[1] unanimously agreed that a core value of any good leader is to treat everyone with respect and dignity. When they said, '*I treat everyone the way I want to be treated*', those were always underlying values they intend to express. That everyone is treated with respect and dignity is an expectation of any healthy group, team or organisation.

The Group of Leaders also noted that leaders, like everyone else, are judged on peoples' *perceptions* of their intention – which may not be the same as their *actual* intention. Perceptions differ depending on peoples' own behavioural preferences, their cultural norms and their beliefs about the leader's intent.

It is important to signal your intent using behaviours that the recipients perceive as equating to what you intend. For example, it is commonly understood that greeting someone respectfully is done differently in Japan and the UK. If you want to indicate your intention of respect when greeting someone from a different culture you are more likely to achieve that by using their normal greeting behaviours.

By using the behaviours the *recipient* thinks signal your intent, you are making it more likely you will be perceived as you intend.

This principle is easiest to understand when working across different geographical cultures. But the principle is also true when working with different businesses or departments within an organisation or different organisations within one geography. It is also true when working with a range of individuals.

As the Emperor Boss knows, the leader must also be capable of shaping what people expect – as individuals and as a group. They must be willing to set standards, norms and expectations where the existing behaviours are not right for the group and its purpose. They must also accept that the people within the group look to them to uphold certain standards and 'rules' for the good of the group as a whole. That is one of the judgements leaders are asked to make as a function of their leadership role.

So when thinking about where to be on the flexibility continuum, an effective leader balances the needs of an individual versus the

[1] The Group of Leaders refers to the 20 successful leaders interviewed whose biographies can be found in the back of the book.

needs of the group as a whole. Then he considers: What is the message I want to convey versus the behaviours that give that message to the recipients?

**The leadership mindset required is 'I treat people in ways they perceive as respectful and in the best interests of the group'.**

THE INSPIRING LEADER

When you think and act in this way you have the mindset of an Inspiring Leader. Operating from this mindset allows you to:

➤ connect positively with a much wider range of people and therefore have more influence with more followers;

➤ communicate your values and principles in ways that are understood and respected by those receiving the message;

➤ align people with the purpose and direction of the organisation without over-prescribing their behaviours;

➤ build greater readiness to listen and act in ways that create trust.

| DILEMMA | DIAGNOSTIC | LEADERSHIP UPGRADE | HOW TO | | |

The Inspiring Leader

The core of good leadership is making decisions that lead to the right outcomes for the group. Inspiring Leaders inspire others in turn to make decisions that are right for their groups.

If you think about what a follower wants in a leader the basics are:

➤ they look competent;

➤ they sound competent;

➤ they are confident and create confidence around them;

➤ they know where they are going and what they want;

➤ they relate in some way to my needs, values and/or aspirations.

Whether you are talking about national leaders or the teenager who leads the fashion in their peer group at school, these conditions are usually being met for their followers.

When you meet these criteria you are able to receive and build 'permission' to lead.

LEADERS

PERMISSION

FOLLOWERS

How can you tell you have permission? The simplest evidence is the level of acceptance you have to make decisions for the group. You may have to make decisions that are both popular and unpopular with individuals and the group, but if the group respects your right to make that decision, then you have permission.

The highly original business thinker Professor Eddie Obeng points out that managers are appointed by their 'superiors', whereas leaders are accepted and even chosen by their followers.[2]

Jack was a very successful salesman in the investment banking arm of a global bank. He was recognised as the top revenue producer and rewarded with very high pay. His direct reports liked working for him because he always vigorously defended them in any disputes with other teams and fought for their reward and promotion. Being very single-minded and driven, he had little time for internal management issues or listening to other colleagues. It was an enormous shock to him to be told in his mid-30s that he would not be promoted to department leader because too many of his peers would resign rather than work for him. They did not trust him to make decisions that were right for the whole group. He had not created permission to take the lead at this higher level.

[2] Obeng, E. (2003) *Perfect Projects*, Beaconsfield, England: Pentacle Works, The Virtual Media Company.

To make decisions that are the right thing for the group, effective leaders are able to:

> understand and communicate a purpose and vision that all the group can sign up to;

> agree and enforce values and behaviours that will enable the group to reach its goals;

> read and relate to the group's needs and individuals' needs;

> balance effectively the group versus individual needs.

These different aspects of leadership are developed further in the next sections.

How to create and communicate the purpose and vision

Groups, like individuals, can perform more effectively together when they have a common sense of purpose and direction.

There are many business books and articles written about creating purpose or vision. Indeed, many works debate which of those words is the right one to use. A much simpler and very useful term encompassing elements of all these ideas can be found in the work of Latitude Consulting.[3] They use the term 'the cause' to mean 'the thing which we get out of bed to do/achieve'. For the rest of this chapter the 'cause' will be used to mean purpose and vision.

Fully effective leaders understand that the cause has to be:

> specific to that group and its context;

> something they can all relate to, sign up to and ideally aspire to;

> independent of any one individual but shared by them all;

> seen as a 'good thing' by all of the group.

One way of thinking about this is to contrast two models of leadership.

---

[3] Latitude Consulting, 'Distinctive characteristics of market-leading companies' www.latitude.co.uk/research.

Leadership based on 'his/her cause'

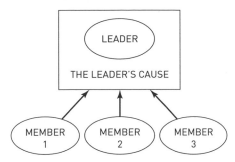

In this model, members of the group may share a common cause, but that cause is actually defined and owned by the leader. Several problems arise from this:

> Individuals have to keep referring to the leader to interpret the cause into correct actions – it is harder for them to 'know' themselves what is the right thing to do.

> Some members only share the cause because they share the desire or need to please the leader – they are only partially motivated.

> If the leader changes, the group experiences no collective direction until a new leader takes control, so energy and momentum dissipates.

> Individual members are less likely to challenge each other or the leader about inconsistent actions or behaviours as they feel dependent on the leader to provide all challenge.

Contrast this with the following model:

Leadership based on 'our cause'

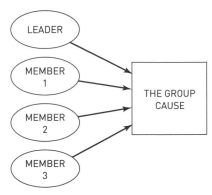

We have to try to find a way where people really charge up about it and know we can get there.[4]

When leadership is based clearly on a shared group cause, performance is higher because:

> ➤ Everyone is motivated by something more satisfying or appealing to them than simply pleasing the leader.

> ➤ Individual members can give healthy challenge to each other *and* to the leader if they see actions or behaviours that do not appear to support the group cause.

> ➤ Individuals feel inspired to do the right things for the group because of their collective ownership of direction and outcomes.

> ➤ Communication tends to work more across the group, rather than up, along and down, allowing more aligned decisions to take place faster.

The leader's role in this model is to understand what the group cause is, or could be. They appreciate it must be shared by the group they are leading and articulated in a way that every member relates to. In modern, fast-moving, or geographically spread businesses, this style of leadership is essential. By creating the group cause for people, the Inspiring Leader inspires others to lead alongside them.

I care that they care and then they make the decisions and they deliver it.

Leaders who lean towards the Hippie Boss style need to focus more on understanding and setting the group cause. They need to ask themselves:

> ➤ *What is (and should be) the core purpose of this group?*

> ➤ *What is so important to this group that they would be willing to alter their own individual needs and behaviours to achieve it?*

On the other hand, leaders who tend towards the Emperor Boss style are good at setting the cause. But before they do so, they need to focus on understanding and engaging with what is motivating and

---

[4] Throughout this chapter there are quotations from the 20 successful leaders who contributed to the book.

relevant to the full range of individuals they lead. In this way they move from creating a top–down 'leader's cause' to a shared 'our cause'.

Good questions here are:

➢ *What underlying interest and purpose do all these people share?*

➢ *How can we express it in ways that are meaningful to all?*

Henry, the finance director on the trading side of a bank, was told by his colleagues in the front office that the finance information produced was too slow, in the wrong format and generally mistrusted. His own team believed they didn't have the right resources and the front office people were too demanding and unrealistic. Resistance to change was high.

Henry got his management team together and asked them to go back to basics: what is the purpose of the finance division? Discussion ranged widely, until they reached a statement they all agreed with: 'Our purpose is to produce high quality, timely information that allows other divisions to make good decisions.'

To their surprise, when the rest of the finance division heard this apparently simple statement they became energised by it. The group, as a whole, wanted to make that statement true. Somehow it touched their collective professional pride and sense of how they contributed to the organisation. After that, barriers to change could be successfully challenged and changes were implemented effectively. Financial information was produced much faster and in ways that met the front office's decision-making needs.

It is important to remember that many facets of a group cause may not be consciously expressed initially. Like an iceberg, much lies below the surface. They are so much a part of the people or organisation that no one would think to mention them. In the finance department's case above, delivering a high

quality, professional service to enable the bank's success was an important goal for everyone but initially seemed too simple.

> *When you do take difficult decisions you do so in a way that is inclusive and bonded and gives people ownership of the outcome.*

One of the best ways to create a shared group cause is to ask leading individuals (and that does not necessarily mean managers alone) to work together to create and express the cause. The leader needs to be an integral but not necessarily dominant part of this work and needs to create both the opportunity and the motivation for people to participate. The leader also needs to ensure that this work continues until the cause is sufficiently clear and can be articulated in ways that people understand and relate to.

When it is 'right' a group cause acts as a thing that resonates and energises members. It becomes a guiding force in future decisions, behaviours and relationships.

Setting and maintaining values, behaviours and expectations

Every group or organisation has a culture associated with it. The culture is an expression of the underlying values and norms of the group, expressed through behavioural customs and practices. This in turn affects how people expect to be treated.

These behavioural norms come from a range of sources such as how leading individuals behaved in the past and the present, the norms of the geographical region and the aspirations of the group.

Successful organisations create and maintain a culture that supports the organisation's cause. It becomes 'our way' of interacting and doing business. It sets people's expectations about how they should behave and can expect to be treated.

For example, if a business has a strategy to be the premium-quality, top customer-service brand in its market, it will be more successful if it has a culture that rewards high attention to detail, pride in satisfying customer needs and refusing to discount its prices to drive volume. Ideally, that culture will in turn attract people who like the business challenges associated with this strategy and have the capabilities to sell this proposition.

Conversely, this culture will not suit salespeople who thrive at managing tight margins across high-volume, low added-service products. Ideally, they will not be attracted into the company, because if they do join they will be at odds with the group's cause and strategy. If they do join the organisation, at best they will not have the opportunity to shine and in all probability they will be a source of constant friction. At worst they may undermine the strategy through constant breaks with 'our way'.

Most cultures can be thought of in three segments as follows:

At the foundation are the *non-negotiables* – the things the organisation as a whole has to comply with to survive and succeed. Individuals and subgroups within the organisation cannot make choices to opt in or out of these behaviours. At a most basic level, complying with the law is a non-negotiable for most (but sadly not all!) organisations. In another context, a rowing team that wants to participate in a four-man rowing contest needs to have four men in a rowing boat at the time of the competition.

The middle segment is made up of the *group-level negotiables* – the things an organisation makes a choice about on the basis of what the group wants, needs and agrees. Individuals are then expected to adhere to these behaviours. In larger organisations, subgroups will have different group-level negotiables, giving variations within the central culture.

Picking up the rowing team example from above, commitment to turn up in time for every practice session may be a non-negotiable for successful four-man rowing teams but different teams will have different group-level agreements about length and frequency of training sessions. Similarly within global organisations, adherence to certain company-wide HR practices may be non-negotiable but different countries may work different hours depending on local working patterns and expectations.

The three culture segments

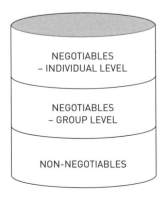

There are some common standards that have to apply. I have little time for people who want to go outside of those.

The top segment is made up of the *individual-level negotiables* – the things an organisation or group agrees can vary by individual. In the case of the four-man rowing team, it may be that every individual is given advice on the best diet to follow but individuals are left to make their own choice whether to follow that diet. In business an organisation may require a certain number of working hours but agree to leave individuals relatively free to decide when to do the actual work.

How much of an organisation's culture belongs in each segment will vary depending on the cause it serves. For example, the armed forces will need, and have, far more non-negotiables than an interior-design business built around an entrepreneur. Utility companies that need to ensure water or electricity is safely available at all times to all customers may require cultures with significantly more non-negotiables and group-level negotiables in place than a start-up dot.com.

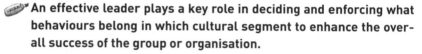 **An effective leader plays a key role in deciding and enforcing what behaviours belong in which cultural segment to enhance the overall success of the group or organisation.**

For example an electricity company may make very high safety standards (higher than legal or regulatory minimums) non-negotiable right across its operations and not just in the more dangerous parts of the business. The leader understands that 'the group' is everyone who comes into contact with the company's business in any way. Success for 'the group' is for everyone to be safe at all times and for all stakeholders to see that in practice.

To ensure it is seen as non-negotiable in the culture the leader must be prepared to clearly sanction or remove those who do not

comply, regardless of how important or valuable they are to the business in other ways. The group looks to the leader to perform that role on their collective behalf. If the leader fails to treat non-compliers in the way the group expects, he creates confusion about what are the real behavioural norms here. This often leads to subsequent pushing of boundaries, increased conflict and loss of trust in the leader.

Steve, a strategy consultant, told me about a successful company he was working with. The company had made a strategic choice to increase its focus on higher value-added, higher-margin products in its marketplace. It made a strategic choice to move away from pushing product through high-volume, low-margin distribution outlets every now and again when expedient.

The new sales director appeared to galvanise the sales team and have all the right connections in the marketplace. However, at the end of his first year, the CEO asked him to leave. When Steve asked the CEO about this he said, 'When the sales team thought they might not make their volume targets he let them push some product through the high-volume discounters again. It threatened overall margins and our whole strategy. No one person, especially a leader in the business, should be behaving in ways that undermine the strategy and the way we have chosen to do business. I'd rather tolerate no sales director for a while than one who's not working in the common interests of us all.'

On the other side of the coin, leaders need to make sure that behaviours applied in the non-negotiable aspects of the organisation don't 'leak' unnecessarily into the more flexible aspects. For example, in a law firm attention to detail is essential in legal documents but may be stifling if translated across to other aspects of the organisation as unwarranted perfectionism.

Leaders tending towards the Hippie Boss behaviours allow too many individual-level negotiables in the culture. Good questions for them to consider are:

➤ *If every individual got to make their own choices on this issue, how would it affect the group's ability to meet its purpose?*

➤ *What are the benefits for other stakeholders when group-level agreements about behaviours are upheld?*

Emperor Bosses need to consider whether the group would be more motivated if some of the non-negotiables the Emperor Boss would like in the culture were replaced by group-level agreements. Questions for them to consider are:

> *What aspects of behaviour and standards could I entrust the members of the organisation to agree themselves?*

> *Where are there decisions where I am not needed and where should I definitely be involved?*

How to read individuals and groups

One of the leader's tasks is to decide whether the group's current culture is best serving the group's cause or whether it needs to change. First he has to read and then lead the culture – but always in keeping with the overall best outcomes for the group.

Good leadership of people requires an acceptance that they will respond to how they perceive your behaviours and not necessarily to what you originally intended.

We all carry in our head presuppositions about how things should be, what certain behaviours mean, how people should behave and what's the right way to do things. We build these presuppositions based on our own experiences, the cultural norms we live in (family, peer group, work, country, religion), and the values we hold. We take in thousands of bits of information over the day and our presuppositions act as necessary filters and short cuts to allow us to respond quickly, and often unconsciously, to the world about us.

Intention and behaviour

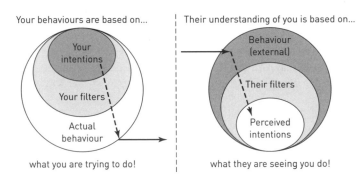

Your behaviours are based on...

Your intentions

Your filters

Actual behaviour

what you are trying to do!

Their understanding of you is based on...

Behaviour (external)

Their filters

Perceived intentions

what they are seeing you do!

For example, when you drive your car on the roads in your home town, you are presupposing that the other drivers will drive on the same side of the road as you.

Fortunately, for most people, most days, this presupposition holds true.

When you are driving in a foreign country, possibly on a different side of the road, you quickly realise you need to change those pre-suppositions! For a period of time you are likely to be cautious while you watch and learn the new rules. When you are comfortable driving in the different territory, you will have become competent in the new 'rules' and increased your flexibility to drive in other unfamiliar territories.

The same is true when you are interacting with a range of people who carry different sets of assumptions and beliefs (filters) on a whole range of issues. This is more obviously of importance when you are leading people across different nationalities and regional cultures. But it also applies with any group of individuals even if they appear similar from the outside!

Everyone's filters are different. Being able to consciously recognise your own and others' for what they are is a prerequisite to being able to expand your ability to read others. It frees you up from assuming too quickly that you understand someone else's intention – or they yours!

Don't take your staff for granted. Understand them well enough to be sure that you deal with each on his own terms.

Accepting that different people carry different filters allows you to appreciate that, if you want to 'treat someone well', then your actions must be consistent with their filters about what equates to being treated well. For example, assume you want to thank and acknowledge someone for making a special effort. Your own preference might be to get a public thank-you in front of an audience and getting 'noticed' in public. But another person's might be a private thank-you and a small personal token, like dinner out with their partner. Yet another person's might be to get 'noticed' by being taken out for dinner by you the leader.

Two vital ingredients that help you read people better are a *desire to connect* and *curiosity*. Curiosity about what 'works' for someone else enables you to increase your ability to influence.

Curiosity is a very valuable tool for leaders.

With due care and sensitivity, a natural human interest in other people on the team is essential.

Being curious is a physiological and mental 'state', like being happy, or energetic, or thoughtful. For leaders, the valuable things about being in a state of curiosity are:

> Your attention is engaged with the person or thing you are curious about – making you more able to connect with what the other person is saying or thinking.

> It supplants disabling mental states such as self-consciousness, anxiety, impatience – making you more focused on what is actually happening in the moment.

> It allows you to suspend temporarily your own presuppositions – making you genuinely more open to the other person's perspective.

> It enables you to listen more openly before making judgements or decisions.

> It enables you to observe whether something is working well or not and learn to adjust to improve results.

You can get into a state of curiosity by vividly remembering previous moments of curiosity or by asking yourself (ideally in a whisper) questions like: *What might they know that I don't?* or *I wonder what I will learn here?* or *What's important for them?*

Alan was the MD of large branded food producer. The job included a great number of internal and external events where Alan had to take a leading role in the 'meet and greet'. Although a confident leader, Alan often felt a little shy in the initial moments of gatherings and found himself wanting to hold back. The breakthrough came when he switched his attention to the people preparing to meet him and got curious about what they might be thinking. He realised many of them, regardless of position, age or experience were probably feeling equally unsure and nervous too. From then on, whenever he noticed himself getting 'shy', he switched his mind to the other person's needs and focused on taking actions to put them at their ease.

Getting curious about other people's mental pictures of the world is an important development for leaders who tend towards the Emperor Boss style. It helps them listen more openly to others' points of view and proposed solutions.

On the other hand, those with Hippie Boss tendencies need to get curious about the wider implications of being agreeable to every individual. It will help them say 'no' where appropriate and explain in a relevant way why certain individual behaviours will not meet the needs of the group as a whole.

Curiosity is also useful when reading the needs of the group as a whole. To start with it is very important to recognise that they are not simply the sum of their individual needs.

When trying to read team needs from team behaviours, a leader has to keep in mind that there may be a number of interpretations for any specific behaviour. To understand which is more likely, they need to create efficient feedback loops. One way is to consult on an informal basis with individuals within the group who are in tune with the group's thinking and will articulate it honestly.

Alternatively, the leader can test what lies behind certain behaviours by considering what they expect to happen in response to particular actions and then taking those test actions.

Key to reading any group is to remember that the group's needs are not simply the net sum of the individual needs. Groups become entities with their own expectations and behaviours.

An effective leader realises they need to work out how to influence at this group level as well as with individuals within the group.

How to balance between group and individual needs

Fully effective leaders understand that a key balancing act is not one of an individual's needs against another, but the needs of an individual versus the group. This simple but very powerful dynamic is captured in Michael Grinder's work on group dynamics.[5]

Grinder uses the three-sided model below to show the interplay between what the group expects and needs from the leader and the leader's effect on the group. Each individual has a relationship with

[5] Grinder, M. *Fundamentals of Group Dynamics*, Battle Ground, WA: MGA Publishers or see www.michaelgrinder.com.

the leader and wants to meet their own needs. The group in turn watches how the leader treats individuals and takes messages from what they see. An effective leader has an eye on both.

The group balancing act

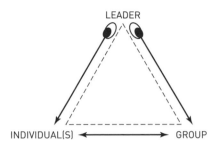

What any one group considers is 'fair' and 'reasonable' will vary even between apparently similar people. Through his many years in education and adult training, Michael Grinder observed that the teacher, being the leader in the room, has to read and adjust their behaviour:

1 between groups; and
2 as the group forms and builds familiarity and/or comfort with each other and the leader.

The leader has to balance the messages he wants to send versus the group's willingness to accept them – hence the need to build permission.

The leader has responsibilities one of which is to call the shots.

When the individual's needs can be accommodated within the group's, leadership choices are relatively easy. The difficulties come when the needs of the individual are at odds with, or are disruptive to, the effective working of the group. In their book *Head, Heart and Guts: How the World's Best Companies Develop Complete Leaders*, Dotlich, Cairo and Rhinesmith[6] point out that choosing between right and wrong is relatively straightforward. Choosing between right and right is the real leadership test.

[6] Dotlich, D.L., Cairo, P. and Rhinesmith, S.H. (2006) *Head, Heart and Guts: How the World's Best Companies Develop Complete Leaders*, San Francisco: Jossey-Bass.

Imagine you are running a bus company and all your customer surveys say that punctuality is the most important part of the service for them. On any one day, all your drivers will face situations where they can see people running up late, hoping the bus will delay for them. If the driver always waits, he may please several individuals, but make the bus late overall – disappointing all the people on that specific bus and the wider group of customers as a whole.

As the leader of the bus company, you could set out a collective policy about what the drivers are supposed to do (i.e. make it a group-level negotiable in your culture). Alternatively, you can leave it to the discretion of each driver to read the situation case by case, having communicated to them clearly the customer priority for punctuality being the key goal. Since customer expectations are largely set by the timetable they are offered, you may also be able to work with your drivers to set a timetable that works best in practice.

It is clear from this example, that the 'right' choice between the individual's needs and the group's needs will be highly context specific. In rural areas, where buses run less frequently, the passengers as a whole may be far more tolerant of waiting for someone who is running up late. Their hope and expectation is that they would be treated the same if it was them. In urban areas, where services are more frequent and time pressures potentially shorter, the collective group of passengers might be less tolerant of delays and expect latecomers to wait for the next bus. In this context they expect and accept that is what will happen to them if they are late. As the leader of the bus company in either context it is your job to read what's best for the group you serve.

Hippie Bosses need to remember that their position as leader confers on them responsibility for shaping and responding to the overall group needs. Sometimes they will have to disappoint an individual to do the right thing for the group. A question to consider is: *If not me, who in the group will set the standards and norms that will create an effective and motivating culture for this group?*

Emperor Bosses need to remember that the members of the group may want greater individual flexibility of behaviour and be willing and able to make that work while still delivering the right outcomes. A question to consider is: *What does the group consider are the right behaviours to motivate and enable us to meet our goals?*

Jonathan was a partner in one of the big four professional services firms. He had just won a very large, complex and publicly visible contract. Getting the right experienced staff was going to be critical to the success of the project and, in turn, the firm's reputation.

Ideally, certain consultants with previous experience would be on the project for 12 to 18 months. But he had a dilemma. There were two or three project managers who would be ideal for the job. In their recent appraisal and development discussions, these individuals had all specifically requested very different work opportunities that year, in order to help broaden their development as future partners. Jonathan could see the needs of the organisation to get the most experienced people on the high-profile project and the needs of the individuals to get broader, career-enhancing opportunities. He was also aware that the whole of his group of consultants would be looking at how he treated the people involved.

In the end he shared his dilemma with the staff involved, making it clear that he expected them to go on the project in some way but asking them how this could be shaped. One was willing to work on the project as long as they got a wider, much more high-profile role. Another agreed to do a few months to kick off on the understanding they would move off it later when a successor was found.

Leaders cannot avoid dilemmas about how to treat individuals and groups. They need to read them well, be respectful of individuals and ensure the best decisions are made on behalf of the group they serve. As with all the leadership dilemmas covered in this book, there will be times and contexts where your leadership style needs to tend towards one end of the flexibility continuum or the other. There are no hard and fast rules. Knowing when and how to change style is what distinguishes an effective leader.

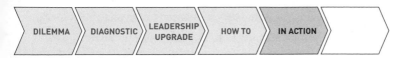

DILEMMA ⟩ DIAGNOSTIC ⟩ LEADERSHIP UPGRADE ⟩ HOW TO ⟩ IN ACTION ⟩

The Inspiring Leader in action

Angela was the leader of a small organisation full of high quality specialists. Her personal leadership style was very open, communicative and responsive to her stakeholders. She herself was totally clear about the organisation's purpose, vision and values and expected those to be understood and shared by everyone in the organisation.

With the strong capability of the people around her, it should have been a high performing team. Instead she saw poor team behaviour, people being difficult with each other and everyone wanting her authority over decisions because they could not persuade colleagues. Clients were not getting the best service. She was spending too much time on day-to-day management, rather than building vital external links. So she stood back to ask: 'What is happening here?' Something in the culture needed to change.

Being an experienced leader, Angela asked herself some questions:

> What's the outcome I want?

> What might the team want to change?

> What are the benefits any change needs to bring for the team, their clients and other key stakeholders – short- and long-term?

> How am I creating or contributing to the problem – explicitly and implicitly?

> How can I motivate the team to make the necessary changes?

Angela raised the issue of the unsupportive culture with the team and made it clear she wanted to change it. Working with an external facilitator, she asked each individual what was causing and supporting the poor team behaviours. She also asked how this culture was affecting their individual and team performance and what each person would do to change things.

The way in which Angela raised this issue reinforced major values she wanted to see in the culture:

> top quality – high performance is expected at all times;
> inclusiveness – each individual is consulted and can contribute;
> honesty – it's important to say what you think;
> openness – willingness to hear feedback good or bad;
> respect – listening to hear the other's point of view;
> accountability – taking responsibility for your actions and their impact.

Once the consultation was complete, the results were shared with the team, 'warts and all'. It was a difficult message, but one which came wholly from the individuals themselves. Angela then asked the whole team (including herself) to work with the facilitator and agree what needed to change in order to create the high-performing team they were capable of being. They were invited to build a common cause around the idea of a high-performing team.

The team agreed a set of behaviours that would lead to higher performance *and* make their working days more effective and satisfying. As leader, Angela set and maintained two key non-negotiables: to be in the team going forward you have to sign up to the high performance behaviours and once the behaviours are agreed everyone will be held responsible for living them.

As a result some significant and very positive changes were made. One person came forward to admit they did not want to work in this way and went on to work for the organisation on a different basis. The rest of the team changed their behaviours and lifted their performance as a whole. All of them understood better their personal impact on their colleagues and accepted their responsibility to be respectful, open and collaborative. More day-to-day decisions are now made within the team, freeing up Angela's time to be a highly effective leader and spokesperson for their work.

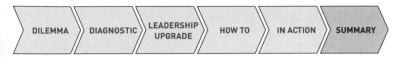
SUMMARY OF KEY POINTS

1 The core of good leadership is making decisions that lead to the right outcomes for the group. Within that context, treating people right is a constant balancing act between meeting versus setting their expectations.

2 The leadership mindset required is: *'I treat people in ways they perceive as respectful and in the best interests of the group'*.

3 Effective leaders build 'permission' to lead from their followers by looking and sounding competent and confident and relating to their followers' needs, values or aspirations.

4 When leadership is based on a shared group cause, performance is higher as people are energised and have a guiding force for future decisions.

5 An effective leader plays a key role in deciding and enforcing which behaviours are non-negotiable, negotiable at the group level and negotiable at the individual level.

6 It is important to signal your intent using behaviours that the recipients perceive as equating to what you intend – to look respectful you must be respectful in their expected way.

7 Curiosity is a very valuable tool for leaders as it enables them to give full attention to others' needs and expectations and reduces the risk of assuming things filtered through their own presuppositions.

8 To read a group's needs it is very important to recognise that they are not simply the sum of their individual needs.

9 A key leadership balancing act is between the needs of the individual and the needs of the group – sometimes that means making a choice between a good thing to do and a right thing to do.

10 The group looks to the leader to uphold the right behaviours, on behalf of the collective good.

Coaching questions

Meeting and managing people's expectations about how they will be treated and what is expected of them is a key part of leadership. This section contains some powerful self-coaching questions to consider.

For suggestions on how to use this self-coaching section see the coaching questions section in Chapter 2.

Building permission

> *What can you do and say that will make people see and hear you as someone who is confident, competent and knows where they are going?*

> *How are you demonstrating that you relate in some meaningful way to your group's needs, values and/or aspirations?*

Creating and communicating 'the cause'

> *What is (and should be) the core purpose of this group?*

> *What is so important to this group that they would be willing to alter their own individual needs and behaviours to achieve it?*

> *What underlying interest and purpose do all these people share?*

> *How can we express it in ways that are meaningful to them?*

> *Who, apart from yourself, are opinion formers who need to be involved in developing and communicating a group cause?*

> *What is the best method and language through which to communicate the group cause?*

> *How will you build feedback loops to check the group cause is understood throughout the organisation?*

Positive culture

> *What are the current non-negotiables, group-level negotiables and individual-level negotiables in the organisation? Are they supportive of the cause?*

- ➤ What, if anything, needs to change?
- ➤ If every individual got to make their own choices on a particular issue, how would it affect the group's ability to achieve the cause?
- ➤ What aspects of behaviour and standards can I entrust the members of the organisation to agree for themselves?
- ➤ Where are there issues where I don't need to be involved and where should I definitely be involved?
- ➤ What are the benefits for stakeholders to know that group-level agreements about behaviours will be upheld?

Reading individuals and groups

- ➤ How well and how often do I listen to others' points of view with a fully open mind?
- ➤ How well do I understand my own filters and presuppositions about how the world should work?
- ➤ How can I increase my ability to understand others' expectations and norms?
- ➤ What feedback loops can I create to understand the individual's and the group's needs better?
- ➤ How can I use curiosity to my advantage?

Balancing between group and individual needs

- ➤ What does the group consider are the right behaviours to motivate and enable us to meet our goals?
- ➤ When I make decisions, what are the needs of and impact on the group as a whole and the individuals?
- ➤ If not me, who in the group will set the standards and norms that will create an effective and motivating culture for this group?
- ➤ How do I manage the desire to be liked versus the need to take potentially difficult or unpopular decisions?
- ➤ How can I build my ability to read situations quickly and flex my response appropriately?

Chapter **5**

....

The delegation dilemma – 'I wouldn't ask someone to do something I wouldn't do myself'

- Highlights (p. 98)
- Delegation – the two extremes (p.98)
- Where do you tend to be? (p.104)
- Balancing wisely (p. 105)
- The Coaching Leader (p.108)
- The Coaching Leader in action (p. 120)
- Summary of key points (p. 122)
- Coaching questions (p. 123)

Highlights

∙∙

➤ In this chapter you will learn how to make delegation simpler, clearer, more compelling and more effective. Delegation is about engaging people positively to make things happen. The art is choosing the right people, asking in the right way and creating clear responsibilities.

➤ Barking Bosses who struggle to let control of tasks go and Superhero Bosses who set big goals with insufficient support both get inferior performance and demotivated teams.

➤ Coaching Leaders delegate successfully by expressing clear outcomes that motivate people. To ensure success they create two-way feedback systems that allow them to seek information and listen well while holding people clearly responsible. At the same time they use acknowledgement to motivate and develop people.

➤ Effective delegation involves playing to people's strengths. This comes from using diversity well and understanding that people perform their responsibilities best if it involves them using skills and talents they have and enjoy using.

DILEMMA

Delegation – the two extremes

Making requests of others is a vital and normal part of leadership. Indeed, the leader cannot set direction without asking others to take action. Effective leaders delegate in ways that engage others to make it happen.

A team of consultants were working on the final report and presentation for a very important client. It was a complex report and they were running very late. Most of the team were going to have to work through the night. The project manager decided he should stay too because he didn't want to look like he was going home and leaving the tough and gritty completion job to others. When his boss heard this she asked, 'What is your role in delivering a great result tomorrow? How does your turning up exhausted and white-faced help the client or the team behind you get the best result?' Seeing the wisdom in her words, the manager checked the team was confident about completing the process by themselves and explained that his role was different to theirs. He needed to go now, get some sleep and then make the best presentation next day of their hard work and great ideas. He also acknowledged their contribution by giving them the next day off and committed to phone and tell them how it went.

Delegation, the art of asking the right person to do things in the right way, is a vital leadership skill. Who to ask and how can be a dilemma.

Like all the leadership dilemmas in this book, there is a range of delegation behaviours. No one style is right for every occasion. At the one extreme, the 'Barking Boss' is like someone who has a dog and does the barking themselves. They are constantly trying to do people's jobs for them. At the other extreme the 'Superhero Boss' sets huge challenges from remote, lofty heights leaving people in a wilderness of confusion and doubt.

THE BARKING BOSS   THE SUPERHERO BOSS

Both are driven by a strong desire for the best results. But they end up creating poorer results by preventing other people from fully contributing their talents.

The Barking Boss's dilemma

The Barking Boss is typified by two common phrases: 'It's quicker to do it myself' and 'If you want a job done well do it yourself.' Both phrases have their time and place but not in the thought processes of effective leaders.

Most Barking Bosses are very capable individuals who like to be very active and 'doing things'. They value people of a similar style. At the same time they are usually over-applying one of four mindsets:

1 The need for speed: 'I'm good at doing this and Fred is not as fast – I'll just do it and he can pick it up some other time.'

2 The need for perfection: 'I know exactly what I want and no one seems to understand or produce that just right so I'll do it myself.'

3 The need to show solidarity: 'I don't like leaving them with this difficult request so I'll stay and help.'

4 Being protective: 'They are already so busy I can't ask them to do more right now.'

Whatever the driver, the results produced by the Barking Boss typically are:

1 A reputation as a micro-manager who frustrates people by never letting them get on with things in their own way. People around them feel resentment at not being able to take ownership of their responsibilities. Others perceive the micro-management as unstated criticism. Such disincentives lead to other capable people avoiding working for a Barking Boss.

2 Very long days filled with a myriad of different tasks and a queue of people waiting for an answer – which apparently only she can give. The Barking Boss becomes a bottleneck everything must go through.

3 People who work for her are robbed of development opportunities, slowing not only their career progression but also that of the Barking Boss herself – she is constantly struggling to develop anyone capable of succeeding her.

4 She ends up hiring people into the team who are very like her – the Mini Me's. Because they think and act like her, she finds it easier to explain things to them and trust them to do things. Over time this lack of diversity stifles innovation and process improvement, reducing the overall effectiveness of her organisation.

The Barking Boss syndrome

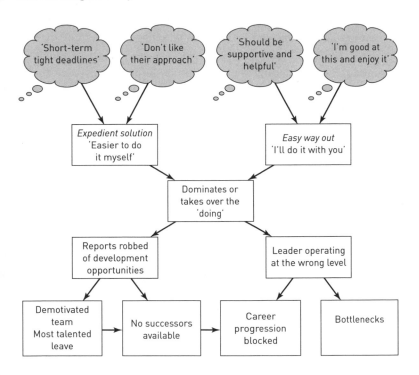

The Superhero Boss's dilemma

The Superhero Boss is focused on huge challenges and making big things happen. She fully embraces the leader's role of setting the direction for others to make things happen. Often, but not always, she is a very high powered individual herself with a strong ability to think conceptually. Followers start by being excited at the ideas and opportunities being presented.

But problems arise for two reasons. The first is the Superhero Boss often lacks the desire to get into too much of the practicalities. This makes her disconnected even from leadership tasks such as ensuring that necessary resources can be found. Being a very challenging and capable individual herself, she creates an aura of superiority around her. This leads to people not wanting to clarify points or raise difficulties.

The second problem arises from a Superhero Boss's tendency to assume other people have the right talents and capabilities for the job. Potentially unaware of her personal talents in certain areas, she assumes everyone else will be as capable as her. She operates from a mindset of 'give people a big challenge and they will rise to the occasion' without really thinking about what support and guidance they will need.

The unintended consequences of this mindset typically are:

1 Superhero Bosses run a high risk of failure. For some people, in some roles or on some projects, she is a fantastic leader giving individuals huge scope and opportunity to shine. But success can be hit-and-miss. The Superhero Boss can be too aloof from the operational details to understand risks in time to react early enough.

2 Followers feel embarrassed or afraid to check their understanding of the expectations, let alone give feedback and/or challenge to the Superhero Boss. So, if things are not crystal clear at the start, there can be a very large mismatch between what was originally expected by the leader and what is delivered by the followers.

3 Second-guessing what she expects becomes the norm rather than effective questioning and dialogue.

4 Direct reports can experience a disabling fear of failure when the Superhero Boss incorrectly assumes that they have all the capabilities and resources needed and the team know they don't. This is compounded if the Superhero Boss fails to listen openly to requests for more or different resources and simply says, 'I'm sure you will find a way through.'

5 Good, talented people are demotivated and leave if they perceive they are being given poorly thought through, ill-matched and high-risk development opportunities without sufficient support.

For a good description of a Superhero Boss in action see Chapter 1 of Martyn Newman's book *Emotional Capitalists.*[1]

The Superhero Boss syndrome

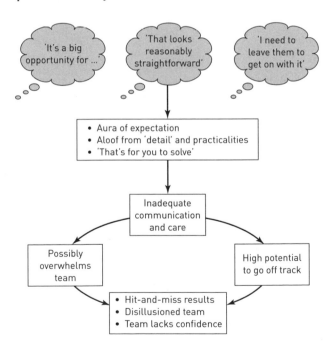

[1] Newman, M. (2008) *Emotional Capitalists: The New Leaders*. Chichester: John Wiley.

Where do you tend to be?

Barking Boss diagnostic

Read the following and assess whether they apply to you. If four or more of these consistently apply it may be time to rethink your delegation style.

1 You can't find people to do tasks properly – the way you would!

2 You end up doing routine work that someone else could do if only you had the time to explain it to them.

3 There are people who do well in your team – but then that's because they think very like you.

4 You regularly have a queue of people at your door wanting decisions on all kinds of things.

5 Your direct reports stop using their initiative and seem to leave it all up to you.

6 Capable people who are self-starters seem to get frustrated and into conflict with you.

7 You regularly exhaust yourself trying to be helpful and keeping everyone on board.

Superhero Boss diagnostic

Read the following and assess whether they apply to you. If four or more of these consistently apply it may be time to rethink your delegation style.

1 You are regularly surprised at the things people seem to have difficulty with.

2 You have some fantastic successes and some unexpected failures.

3 Things can go significantly off course before you become aware of the problems.

4 Some people surprise you by appearing paralysed from taking action when you thought everything was clear.

5 People seem afraid to ask you questions and clarify things.

6 People seem reluctant to push back or open dialogue with you when they disagree, leading to wasted effort.

7 People are less pleased with the development opportunities you create for them than you expected.

In this chapter you will learn how to make delegation simpler, clearer, more compelling and more effective.[2]

Balancing wisely

Using the talents of yourself and others well is a skill and habit of good leaders. An essential leadership task is choosing the right people to do specific roles and making sure they understand what they must deliver. Fully effective leaders develop the skill, processes and curiosity to understand different people's strengths and skills and engage them to best use. For them, delegation is about ensuring the people with the right capabilities are asked to do appropriate roles – roles where they can express their talents positively and successfully.

[2] There is also a simple, effective delegation 'audit' available on the website, **www.badgerordoormat.com**.

The ability to delegate is the ability to find someone and trust them to do it their way – not your way. It's what they produce that counts.[3]

Barking Bosses struggle to let go of doing activities themselves. They often want to 'help' by doing it themselves or telling someone how to do the job – usually their way! Their focus is strongly on the activity and not the outcome. They put 'getting things done' ahead of building and using everyone's capabilities most effectively to deliver great outcomes.

Sue, a sought-after speaker and trainer, knew she needed an assistant to do the administrative work around her. But each time she hired someone to do the job she was frustrated at how much explaining she had to do and how long it took the assistant to do things. As a result she kept diving in and doing things that she could do quicker and more efficiently herself. This in turn confused the assistant who ended up constantly having to ask what was happening with each task. Frustration was high all round.

Sue decided this pattern had to stop. She started to delegate by explaining the outcome she wanted more clearly and then asking and welcoming open questions to allow the assistant to get fully clear. She then let go of the need to watch over the process and focused herself on what she was best at – being with clients. Her assistant grew in confidence to become faster and developed her own ways of doing things quickly and efficiently.

Some Barking Bosses fear being seen to leave others to do 'the dirty work'. However, if you start to explore that, you quickly realise there is usually a flaw in that thinking. Imagine the leader of a construction firm who had a strong personal dislike of working on roofs. If he thinks of roofing as 'the difficult and dirty work', he clearly might struggle to ask others to put roofs on the buildings – not a very effective mindset! The leader will get a very different result if he is clear that roofing is a necessary task to be done and then hires

[3] Throughout this chapter there are quotations from the 20 successful leaders who contributed to the book.

people who are willing to do roofing. Better still, he looks for people who enjoy that part of the job.

➤ **Fully effective leaders understand their own limitations and don't let them become limitations on the organisation they lead.**

The Superhero Boss is disconnected with the realities of what she is asking. For example, she might ask someone to organise an event to bring certain parties together to resolve an issue. Thinking that the way to do this is obvious, she may not check that the person she has asked fully understands the delicate nature of the discussions and the potential risks of things going wrong. She may not even check whether they have any experience in running this type of event. A better approach would have been to look at who has talents in building relationships and handling conflict, brief them fully on the outcomes required and ask them what challenges they see ahead.

> *When the light goes on with someone, they think it is their idea and they will go off and do it. The pay-off is it frees up your time.*

The other enormous benefit leaders get from good delegation is time to think for themselves. This vital change from doing to reflecting and thinking can be scary at first. But when you achieve this change, you realise the enormous benefit that time for reflection brings to a fully effective leader.

➤ **The leadership thinking required is 'I ask people to do things they have the capability and resources to do'.**

When you engage people with a task in ways that make their work interesting, challenging, or meaningful to them, you get much more of their specific talents and skills expressed and much higher performance.

One of the key ways to create this engagement through delegation is to become a Coaching Leader. Let go of the desire and need to do the job yourself. Stay in touch through regular, supportive conversations around:

THE COACHING LEADER

> the outcomes expected;
> the resources needed (including training and development);

> the results being achieved;

> the possibilities that could lead to greater success yet.

In this way, they engage people's talents and motivation and can hold them to their delegated responsibilities.

The Coaching Leader

All effective leaders want to get the best results for their stakeholders. In this chapter, we look at how a Coaching Leader creates the right environment for good delegation by:

> being clear about the outcomes expected;

> selecting people with the right talents and capability for a task;

> using diversity to increase performance;

> acknowledging people;

> giving and seeking feedback;

> managing accountability.

As one of the Group of Leaders said, *'Delegation is a very good way of motivating people. Agree with them what needs doing and then let them get on with it. Take an interest but don't ride on their backs all the time'.*

How to set outcomes

Creating clarity about the outcomes expected is key. Think how much more productive you are when you know exactly what you are aiming for. When a leader can create this clarity in the minds of many followers, they increase the productivity and sense of satisfaction for everyone. They can even motivate people to do all the mundane tasks that just need to be done. One of the greatest enemies of clarity is taking insufficient time to communicate and check understanding with your followers.

Coaching Leaders utilise coaching techniques for outcome-setting. They start by being very clear about what they want. They express goals and expectations in terms of tangible things they will see or hear happening when the goal is achieved. For example, instead of simply stating 'the business must grow by 5% this year', they might express that as 'I am looking forward to seeing a new branch of the business opened next year as a result of growing the business by 5% this year'. This change automatically allows other people to engage with the goal by connecting them to tangible future events. (For more on communication see Chapter 3.)

Ideally, the leader will also test the understanding of their follower(s) by asking questions about what they expect to see, hear or feel when the outcome has been achieved. For example, the leader might ask: 'What do you see as being the key things that will be different as a result of growing by 5% this year?' and 'What will it allow us to do?' People can relate much better to a 'story about how the future will be' rather than a set of figures or statistics you desire to make true.

It is important to bear in mind the difference between an 'output' and an 'outcome'. Taking an example from politics and looking at the diagram below, we note that the public wants the *outcome* of any interaction with the medical profession to be a fast, effective and convenient resolution of their health issue. Politicians see the *need* for health services that can deliver that outcome. They then require health officials to meet certain targets, e.g. length of waiting time for operations. These targets become *outputs* that get measured.

The *outcome* is the big picture objective. The *outputs* are specific success measures that ideally, when met, will mean the desired outcome has been achieved. The *tasks* are the things being done to deliver the outputs.

A vital question is always: are those outputs actually delivering the outcomes needed and expected?

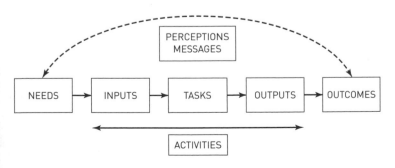

Understanding the needs and desired outcomes of stakeholders and ensuring that the outputs are addressing these well is an important leadership role. Communication plays a big part in this. The leader needs to make sure there is continuous good dialogue to establish clearly the expectations and outcomes, and keep people informed of progress toward these.

Another important facet of outcome-setting is to be able to answer the questions: *'Why are we doing this? What will the benefits be? What will it do for us?'* The answers to these questions give followers context for the work to be done and engagement with the purpose. Both will increase their motivation and final satisfaction. Going back to our business example, the leader might say, 'Achieving the 5% growth target will give us sufficient revenues to maintain our staff bonuses and invest in new, brighter offices', or 'Achieving 5% growth will let us continue to attract and retain sufficient investment to develop our new product pipeline and retain customers.'

John, a coach who had been a finance director in a charity, once told me: 'If I had had the alignment with my corporate goals that I have now I would have achieved so much more.' When asked what was different he said, 'Now my goals are expressed in outcomes that are meaningful and motivating to me. I can really see and hear the things I want to happen, making me far more prepared to do what it takes to make them happen.'

Always express goals in the positive. Avoid measurement systems that are expressed in the negative. For example, use 'we remain a team in the first division' rather than 'we avoid relegation'.

Finally, it is important to review the possible impact of the goal(s) on key stakeholders in your world. Understanding how other parties, such as staff, investors and competitors, may respond to your ambitious plans is a vital part of setting well-formed goals. A Coaching Leader ideally has this conversation with her managers and staff, engaging them in the process of goal-setting. Ultimately it creates their buy-in to the responsibility they are being delegated.

How to match the person to the task

Picking the right team around you has been a well recognised aspect of good leadership across the history of mankind. In his book *Good to Great*[4] Jim Collins gives a very cogent set of arguments as to why this is an essential leadership skill and task. His research shows that matching the right people with the right skills and attitude to each role is key to success. Those people then formulate the right way to go and make it happen.

This section focuses on how to match people's capabilities to the task.

People are far more likely to take and perform well at delegated responsibilities if they can use the capability, skills and talents they have and enjoy. Recall a working day when you come home thinking you have had a really good day. The chances are you have been engaged in activities that you not only excel at but also enjoy and which energise you. What would be the difference in productivity and satisfaction if most of your team went home from work most days feeling like that?

Effective leaders take time to understand and appreciate people's capabilities, skills and talents – their own included. They also help others to recognise and develop their capabilities.

Two approaches that are particularly useful for analysing people's strengths are Martin Seligman's signature strengths framework[5] and Dan Sullivan's unique abilities[6] model.

Seligman defines 'a strength' as a trait that is valued in its own right because its use produces desirable, satisfying results. Typically, they are characteristics that parents would wish for their children such as courage, love of learning and integrity. An important feature of strengths is that they can be developed in an individual.

[4] Collins, J. (2001) *Good to Great*, London: Random House Business Books.
[5] Seligman, M. (2003) *Authentic Happiness*, London: Nicholas Brealey Publishing.
[6] Nomura, C. and Waller, J. (2006) *Unique Ability: Creating the Life You Want*, Toronto: The Strategic Coach Inc.

The signature strengths framework identifies 24 separate strengths. Most people will possess several of these (their 'signature') which, when they use them in any realm of their lives, create energy and enthusiasm, a sense of authenticity and a desire to find more ways to use them. When we are working in ways that use our signature strengths we are most likely to experience a sense of 'flow' – being so engaged in something that we become unconscious of our emotions and of time.

The starting point of Dan Sullivan's unique abilities approach is that each of us has a set of skills, capabilities and personal qualities, which combine together to give us unique abilities in certain areas of activity. They are not just learnt skills but a combination of specific capabilities and attributes that give a person a clear advantage as well as pleasure in doing certain tasks. For example, someone who is 'a good presenter' may be using a range of capabilities such as the ability to understand other people's expectations in combination with creating imaginative visuals and clear, simple messages.

In this model, you differentiate your 'abilities' on the basis of both the quality of the results you produce and the emotion it engenders in you. Unique abilities involve activities that you have superior capabilities to do and which you love doing. On the flip side, there are activities you do which cause you high stress and frustration while still only producing poor results – these are labelled your 'incompetents'.

In both Seligman's and Sullivan's frameworks, the key message for leaders is that delegation will be much more effective when the task engages a person's strengths or talents in a positive way for them and the organisation.

The leader of a relatively small organisation got everyone to apply the unique abilities principles to their current jobs. Each individual worked with three to four close colleagues to agree their unique abilities. Then, as a team, they looked at what each person's current job entailed and the extent to which they were able to make use of these unique abilities.

Two big mismatches emerged. The person best suited to handling the media was doing less of this activity than others. Also two of the support staff were doing generalist jobs when they each had strong abilities and preferences for doing different specific parts of their combined jobs. With some quick renegotiation of roles, the team swapped around certain tasks. As a result four people found themselves with much more interesting and fulfilling roles. Overall team productivity increased as a result.

All development requires people to move out of their comfort zone for a while. When they are using their strengths and talents they will respond positively to this stretch and challenge, and expand their comfort zone as a result. Leaders need to observe, encourage and, on occasion, take risks with delegation to build capability in their organisation.

Actually people are flattered to be asked to do something they perceive as breaking new ground.

At times, people will have the capability and talent but need actual skills training to express that capability effectively. Training and development are one type of resource that fully effective leaders ensure is available to people. You will get far greater value investing your training budget not on taking people from incompetent to competent, but in supporting people to develop the talents and strengths they get satisfaction from using.

How to use diversity to drive performance

Using diversity well in organisations is not just about gender, age and ethnicity. Acknowledging the differing talents in your followers and matching them wisely to the tasks and challenges is an excellent route to collective higher performance.

Fully effective leaders build a diverse team with a range of strengths and talents suited to the tasks and challenges the group or organisation faces. For example, to set up a new business division, the leader may choose someone who thrives in an uncertain environment, can hold and articulate the big picture and be very persuasive. If the leader also recognises that the individual is not very strong at practical organisation, they can propose another team member with this talent to balance the team.

Effective delegation is about playing to people's strengths. Far more can be achieved by a team where each person's strengths and weaknesses are acknowledged and used to inform decisions about who does what.

A leader can stand in the way of teamwork or they can facilitate it, encourage it and utilise effectively the processing power of the whole team.

For example, winning quiz teams usually have members with a diverse range of knowledge, interests and ages. Just as importantly, winning teams know which person they are relying on for the answer to different types of questions – and they hold each other accountable!

The reality is that a leader will have many people working for them who will be much more talented at certain things. Importantly, those other people will enjoy doing those tasks far more than the leader would. Many of the Group of Leaders talked about how important it was to appreciate this fact and therefore learn to hire highly talented (and often challenging) people round them.

Get people better than you and build a strong team round you.

Being fair The Group of Leaders had two main points to make about being fair when asking people to do things for the organisation.

The first was that people should be given the right equipment, resources and training to do the job properly – from top executives to the people cleaning the toilets.

You need to be fair and reasonable in your requests of people and where appropriate demonstrate to their satisfaction that there is a good reason for what you are asking them to do.

The second point made by the Group of Leaders was that sometimes a leader has to ask someone to do something that is difficult or potentially very tough. Some organisations, such as the armed forces, clearly ask people to do things that are dangerous. One corporate example was an organisation wanting to open an office in a less developed country. The person ideally suited to do this job had a family and the country was relatively inhospitable for families. They would need to live apart from their family for periods of time.

In these types of circumstance the questions the leaders ask themselves are:

> Is there a strong and valid reason for asking this specific person to do this – valid in terms of the organisation or the purpose and people we serve?

> If I were similarly capable, talented and situated, would I be willing to do this myself in the circumstances?

> Have we given due consideration to all the risks and how these might best be mitigated or controlled?

How to give acknowledgment and feedback

Throughout this chapter the word 'acknowledge' is deliberately used many times. The dictionary definition of acknowledge is 'to agree to the truth of' and 'recognise the authority or claim of' as well as 'to express appreciation of'.

Acknowledgement is a vital ingredient of motivation. Research by the Corporate Leadership Council[7] looked at the factors that produced the highest gains in individual performance. The most effective performance enhancer was fair, accurate, informal feedback from a trusted source – usually the boss. When done well, this potentially raises performance by up to 40%.

Feedback that emphasised performance strengths was shown to be a major performance enhancer – up to 36%. Feedback that only emphasised weakness in employee performance and was not grounded in specific feedback for improvement, reduced performance by up to 26%.

[7] The Centre for Corporate Leadership (2007) *Improving Talent Management Outcomes*, Washington DC.

Acknowledgement of someone's strengths is a useful way to make a connection with them and create their positive engagement with their job.

What is acknowledgement? For starters it is more than praise. Praise is great to receive. It signals the giver's approval of someone's behaviour such as, 'Well said. I am proud of you.' Praise is usually phrased from the giver's perspective – it is about what they think.

One way to be a better Coaching Leader is to learn to acknowledge something meaningful about the person. For example 'The leadership you showed when you spoke up lifted the meeting.' When the acknowledgement 'lands' with the recipient they internally recognise something about themselves. They feel known. Acknowledgement is recognition of who they are rather than what they have done. The attention is on the recipient's thinking and who they are. Giving this deeper acknowledgement increases the Coaching Leader's ability to connect people with their own talents and how to develop them. It also helps the person see how they can be successful again in the future.

Interestingly, even acknowledgement of potentially less attractive sides to someone's persona can be accepted as positive recognition of 'who I am' if the recipient has accepted these qualities in themselves already.

Leaders make delegation more effective and motivating when they link what someone is being asked to do to with acknowledgement of that person's qualities.

Getting accurate and timely feedback so you can 'stay in touch' is another vital part of delegation. How frequently you should ask for reports and feedback varies with the individual and the situation. Clearly you will want to be informed more regularly when delegating to someone less experienced or when the task is very critical to the organisation.

You have to find a way of knowing it is alright without knowing everything.

Effective leaders develop their ability to stay in touch by informally coaching their reports. In this context coaching means having a dialogue that helps the person think through challenges rather than telling them the answer. Using a coaching approach, the leader gets to hear and influence how someone is thinking and behaving without directing and/or demotivating them. The person reporting gets a valuable opportunity to get fresh perspective and feedback without feeling overly judged and directed.

> **Followers like working for Coaching Leaders who enable them to use and develop their strengths and abilities and are willing to coach and offer feedback at appropriate times.**

> Tim, a manager in a software firm, told me that he really liked working for his current boss. He said, 'You can go and talk something through with him and get his perspective without him taking over the issue or making the decision for you.'

An important facet of a coaching approach is to come to it with an open mind and genuine curiosity (for more on the state of curiosity see Chapter 4). Your primary objective is to help them think about their issues in a way they find useful so they will continue to open up to you in the future.

Ask open questions and probe with care any issues you have concerns about. Questions asked with genuine curiosity are far less threatening to the recipient and increase the possibility of widening their thinking – and your own!

> Nick, a senior finance executive, received feedback that he was sometimes seen as negative and stubborn with people. It turned out that he enjoyed tough debate around an issue and liked to hold his ground until convinced. He did not intend to put people off talking things through with him. In response to the feedback, he changed his style by using open questions. He became being much more curious about the differences in thinking between himself and the other person. As a result, he found his questions often helped people to recognise aspects of an issue they had missed. More importantly, people found the conversation with him helpful rather than difficult.

Other good sources of feedback come from listening well to the formal and informal messages coming from other observers, participants, customers and suppliers. Effective leaders are constantly curious to know 'how we are doing' and value feedback enormously. One aspect of getting such feedback is to create ways of gathering information from several different sources and cross-checking them.

Effective formal and informal review processes are crucial if people are to take responsibility for the outcomes they have been delegated. There is a large volume of thinking available covering performance review processes and giving feedback so this will not be covered further here except for one aspect – culture.

The leader and leadership team play a vital role in setting the right culture to make meaningful performance reviews happen. Influencing culture around feedback requires a realistic understanding of the way the organisation works and a strong commitment to model the feedback and accountability culture they want. (For more on deciding to create change in an organisation see Chapter 6.)

Take, for example, a business that wants to improve performance review discussions. The objective is to ensure employees know openly what they are valued for and where they need to change or develop going forwards. For this to happen, the leadership team needs to ensure they create this quality of performance dialogue with their own direct reports, whether formally or informally, and that this is tangible to the organisation.

> The head coach of the London Wasps Rugby Club explained to me how they use feedback and coaching to maintain a high performance culture. After each match, each player goes through video clips with different coaches looking at every part of the game where they had a role: kicking, line-outs, scrums, etc. The player and the coach analyse what they do well and what they could do better and create an action plan for that week's practice training and the next match. Attendance at your coaching sessions is voluntary, but any drop in performance can cost you your place in the team. Several of the top team players assured me they did not miss their feedback and

coaching sessions. They understood they needed to constantly improve to stay at the top and they were setting an example to the junior players in the club.

How to manage accountability

There was strong consensus amongst the Group of Leaders that leaders must hold others responsible for delegated areas of activity but the leader remains ultimately accountable for their organisation and its activities.

If you delegate something you don't abandon it. You give someone authority to do it, but you must check to see what they've done.

Holding people to their promises is made easier if the outcomes expected were clearly understood and were motivating for the delegatee. Thinking through and agreeing tangible milestones and success measures at the start gives the leader clear pointers as to whether results are on track later.

If a leader wants to create a high performance culture, they must be prepared to take necessary actions when things go wrong. This could be someone repeatedly failing to deliver or regularly behaving in ways that are not in line with the values and standards expected. This is a time when leaders must accept the responsibility of their positional power. They need to take action to uphold the standards and behaviours they and others expect.

Ultimately people look to the leader to take tough decisions on behalf of the whole group (managing the group versus managing the individual is covered in Chapter 4). She must constantly be aware that the way in which she deals with poor performance will be closely watched. She will need to decide how strong and how public to make punitive actions. Followers and other stakeholders will consider if the actions are 'fair' and 'reasonable' and what the message is. Ideally leaders will consult, usually informally, before taking actions but they must take ownership of the final decision.

DILEMMA › DIAGNOSTIC › LEADERSHIP UPGRADE › HOW TO › IN ACTION ›

The Coaching Leader in action

The Coaching Leader in action is illustrated by the story of Jennifer. Jennifer was the national director of a large charity responsible for the care of people with intellectual disabilities. The charity operated through five regional organisations and Jennifer's national role was to liaise with the governing board, champion charity-wide initiatives and ensure cohesion of approach, standards and ethos.

In response to changes in funding sources and the desire for greater transparency of governance, the board decided to change the governance arrangements. Each region was to report to a newly created regional board, with board members coming from the local community. Jennifer would become national chief executive with an executive team made up of the regional directors. Jennifer was charged with putting these arrangements into practice.

Through coaching, Jennifer had developed a much better appreciation of her own strengths and unique abilities. These included a deep respect for individuals' needs, a strong desire to reach out and connect people to work together, and an ability to hold tenaciously to big-picture goals and outcomes while dealing with necessary nitty-gritty process issues. She enjoyed meeting new people, finding new ways of doing things better and was not afraid to push to get things done when necessary.

Working with her coach, Jennifer asked, 'What do I have to do to be a good chief executive?' They talked through the idea that different types of leadership were required for different periods in an organisation's life. Jennifer's organisation was about to go through a major change that would take several years to complete and would affect many stakeholders. The coach asked her to think through and list out all the qualities and traits desirable in someone who is CEO of the organisation during this period of change.

When she completed her list, Jennifer realised, with some surprise, how closely her own abilities matched those she would want in a leader during this major change. She also recognised explicitly something that was just a feeling before: the changes would not be successful unless the regional directors and staff fully bought in. This would require them to be involved and consulted, despite their desire to just 'get on with their day job' and stay away from the change process.

With this new insight and appreciation of the value of her own talents, Jennifer went about the change confidently. She looked at the unique abilities she saw in people around her and delegated them roles in the change project that suited their abilities and interests. In this way she got people doing the things they found easiest and most interesting, thereby reducing resistance.

When the time came to recruit new regional board members, Jennifer recognised her own talents at engaging with new people and helping them find ways to work together. She emphasised proper induction processes and communication to create clarity of common purpose.

The change process took longer than everyone originally expected and had to deal with many unexpected issues. When things got difficult or slow, Jennifer used her talent to tenaciously hold on to the big picture. She coached herself and others to focus on the need for change and the better organisation being created for the people they served. She also helped herself and others to have enormous patience by being continuously respectful of other people's positions and needs, even in the face of disagreement and setbacks. Jennifer was the change leader her organisation needed because she used her own and others' talents wisely.

The organisation now has fully operational regional boards that are functioning well. Jennifer is focused on creating, with the senior regional leaders, national level strategy and policy which guide local plans and implementation.

DILEMMA 〉 DIAGNOSTIC 〉 LEADERSHIP UPGRADE 〉 HOW TO 〉 IN ACTION 〉 SUMMARY

SUMMARY OF KEY POINTS

1 The leadership thinking that supports fully effective delegation is: *'I ask people to do things they have the capability and resources to do'.*

2 Choosing talented people and matching them to tasks wisely is a key leadership skill.

3 The benefit of effective delegation is that it engages people's skills, talents and emotional involvement. It allows them to express their capabilities. It also gives you, the leader, more time for thinking and communicating.

4 Delegation starts with being very clear about the outcomes expected. Measures of success and the benefits to be delivered should be tangible and meaningful to those delivering them.

5 Understanding different individuals' capabilities and talents is a key part of good leadership as using those capabilities will be motivating and energising for them. It can help to think in terms of 'What does this person excel at and love to do?'

6 Leaders need to be clear about their own capabilities, talents and areas of weakness and ensure they do not let these limit others or the organisation itself.

7 Effective delegation and use of diversity is about playing to people's strengths. Far more can be achieved by a team where each person's strengths and weaknesses are acknowledged and used to inform decisions about who does what.

8 A coaching approach with followers allows leaders to be supportive and stay in touch with progress without demotivating people.

9 Fully effective delegation includes making sure people have access to the right resources. Training is an important resource alongside manpower, budget and equipment.

10 Acknowledgement through recognition of a person's capabilities and contribution is a key way to engage someone and get higher performance.

11 Leaders who demonstrate effective feedback processes and hold people accountable create a performance-oriented culture.

12 Leaders should always hold others to their delegated responsibilities but remain accountable overall.

Coaching questions

A key skill for leaders is delegating in ways that are motivating and engage people with their goals and tasks. The art of delegation is a balance between being too hands-on and too remote. When reading this chapter you may find there are specific areas where you may want to change and improve. These powerful self-coaching questions are grouped into areas for consideration.

For suggestions on how to use this self-coaching section see the coaching questions section in Chapter 2.

Understanding yourself

➢ *What types of people do I feel most comfortable delegating to? What is it about them I value?*

➢ *What types of people am I least comfortable delegating to? What is it about them that concerns me?*

➢ *What types of activities do I love doing because I find them easy, energising and satisfying?*

➢ *What things or activities do others think I am really good at, and ask me/pay me to do for them?*

➢ *What do I hate doing, find frustrating and produce poor results at?*

Setting outcomes

➤ *How can I express clearly the outcome(s) I want/require? Write down your outcomes in terms of clear, positive, tangible things that others will be able to see or hear happening.*

➤ *Is it clear 'why we are doing this' and 'what the benefits will be', in terms that are meaningful to the people doing the tasks?*

➤ *What are the outputs that will lead to the outcomes wanted?*

➤ *What type of response might we expect from other stakeholders? Will that affect our ability to achieve our goals?*

Assessing others

➤ *What does the person love to do, does with ease and always does well?*

➤ *When offered choice, where do they focus naturally? What is the underlying capability or value being expressed?*

➤ *What does the person hate doing, avoid doing and usually do poorly? What would they publicly own up to not being good at?*

➤ *What sources have I used to gather data about them? Who else could give me insights (including the person themselves)?*

➤ *What do I acknowledge and appreciate about them?*

Matching people and tasks

➤ *What aspects about a task make me choose one set of talents in preference to another?*

➤ *Will the person feel acknowledged or valued in some way or see an opportunity for satisfaction for them?*

➤ *Are there any tasks the organisation or team needs to do where we do not have people with the right talents?*

➤ *What further resources (money, people, time, training) does the person need to be successful?*

Overseeing

> *What style and frequency of communication will give me and my report sufficient comfort and control?*

> *What are the core things that matter and which our dialogue should focus on? Are we both clear what those are?*

> *Am I asking questions that help them think things through and succeed? Or questions that help me feel in control?*

> *How can I maintain open and positive dialogue so they can be open with me?*

> *When and from where can I collect other informal feedback to keep me informed?*

> *How can I express acknowledgement of what they do and are doing well? What would they feel proud of?*

> *How comfortable am I with holding people accountable?*

> *If not comfortable, what steps can I take to make it easier?*

> *Am I modelling for the organisation the performance-oriented behaviours I want to be happening everywhere?*

Chapter **6**

The change dilemma – 'If it ain't broke don't fix it'

- Highlights (p. 128)
- Initiating change – the two extremes (p. 128)
- Where do you tend to be? (p. 133)
- Balancing wisely (p. 134)
- The Driving Leader (p. 137)
- The Driving Leader in action (p. 155)
- Summary of key points (p. 157)
- Coaching questions (p. 158)

Highlights

➢ In this chapter you will learn how to evaluate the need for change, assess the organisation's capability for change and the right timing.

➢ Tortoise Bosses are unwilling to start change unless they have to for fear of painful mistakes. Runaway Bosses constantly start change regardless of the chaos it may cause. Both get into a downward spiral. Too little change, too slow, leads to dangerous mediocrity. Too many changes initiated but not completed leads to overwhelm, frustration and low performance.

➢ Driving change is one of the primary responsibilities for any leader. The leadership thinking required is 'Could it be better – and how?' Deciding what to change, when to change and building commitment from the group needs care and requires the leader to balance many conflicting factors.

➢ Effective change decisions begin with clarity of objective, understanding the issues from multiple perspectives and balanced assessment of a broad range of costs, benefits and risks. Successful leaders assimilate this information into a clear decision-making process and enable others to buy in through understanding the change drivers for themselves.

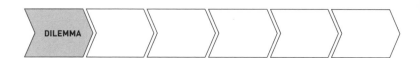

DILEMMA

Initiating change – the two extremes

Change is an essential part of an organisation's survival and growth. Smart organisations change before the external environment forces them to because they know it is easier to change from a position of strength. They also know change takes time to flow through – giving yourself sufficient time leads to greater chance of success. But change has costs associated with it. Too slow to start change and the organisation stagnates. Too much change leads to initiative overload.

Tom was an ambitious and hard-working finance director. Less than a year into the job, he could see many areas where his department could be improved. At the same time, he was constantly being pulled into meetings with his internal customers about project delays and poor delivery. His staff complained to him that they were exhausted with the endless change as nothing seemed to get completed. Before any change had a chance to deliver benefits, it was superseded by another one. Tom realised something was going wrong.

He sat down with his senior team and agreed what the key priorities were. Some changes would have to wait or be cancelled. They then agreed the priorities with their internal customers on the basis that this smaller number of key projects would be delivered on time and budget in the future. The result was higher overall performance as the team and the customers could focus, staff jobs were more satisfying and the business experienced the benefits.

Initiating the right change at the right time to drive success for the group or organisation is a key leadership function.

This chapter focuses on the dilemma of deciding what to change and when. It does not focus on leading the implementation of change itself. For further reading on change see Kotter and Cohen's *The Heart of Change*.[1]

THE TORTOISE BOSS   THE RUNAWAY BOSS

[1] Kotter, J.P. and Cohen, D.S. (2002) *The Heart of Change: Real-life Stories of How People Change Their Organizations*, Boston: Harvard Business School Press.

At one extreme we have the Tortoise Boss, unwilling to make changes unless she really has to. At the other end of the continuum we have the Runaway Boss, constantly starting new initiatives before previous ones have been completed and can show benefits.

Both want the best for their organisation. But, unwittingly, both are creating conditions that hamper the performance of that organisation.

The Tortoise Boss's dilemma

The Tortoise Boss knows that change is necessary but also can be disruptive and distracting for an organisation. So her response is to take decisions about change very slowly and carefully.

Several reasons may lie behind the Tortoise Boss's over-cautious approach:

> She may simply like to get everything absolutely clear with all the analysis and evidence lined up and the plan buttoned-down tight before she will say 'yes' to going ahead.

> She may have 'scars' from previous changes that leave her unwilling to risk potentially painful decisions and disruption.

> She may simply be blind to or resistant to changes in the business environment that do not fit with her internal picture of how things are or should be.

> She may have had considerable success with a particular approach in the past and be struggling to see the need to change it.

The Tortoise Boss's positive intention is to get any change absolutely right. Good decision making combines instinctive ideas, clear analysis and consultation. But persistently initiating change too slowly can lead to the following negative consequences.

1 The organisation/team ends up constantly playing catch-up against the best in the market and gets a reputation of being middle-ranking and mediocre.

2 The organisation's ability to change becomes increasingly paralysed either with endless analysis in search of absolute certainty or general indecision creating lack of direction.

3 Challenge, innovation and listening to people's instincts are not actively encouraged. People who like and thrive on change don't stay long with the team as they see very little development opportunity.

4 The team members who are left learn to stay within their comfort zone and do not challenge themselves to reach higher standards, so change becomes harder.

As a leader you have to be prepared constantly to destroy what you have built and that is very difficult because you are so proud of what you have built.[2]

The Tortoise Boss spiral

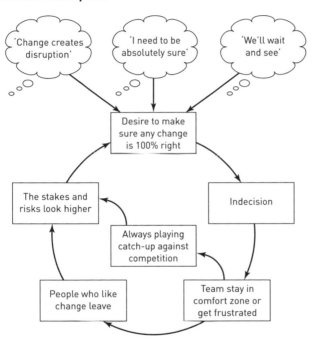

The Runaway Boss's dilemma

The Runaway Boss can always see bigger, better, faster ways of doing things. Often she is someone who is very tolerant of change herself or indeed thrives on it. She is very open to external feedback and quickly translates that into things that need to be done differently.

Runaway Bosses throw out a constant stream of potentially unconnected ideas which, in turn, become new change initiatives.

[2] Throughout this chapter there are quotations from the 20 successful leaders who contributed to the book.

As a result, the team or organisation around them experience constantly changing plans and priorities. After a while the organisation starts to experience overwhelm and performance suffers.

Initiating many changes rapidly may be a necessary response in certain market conditions or when the organisation is in start-up or rapid turnaround. But many times, when one wave of change quickly replaces another, it results in the following situations.

1 Nothing gets completed before it is abandoned, so the expected benefits of each change are not achieved but a lot of the costs are incurred.

2 Individuals work very hard but the performance outcome does not reflect their effort and this leaves them feeling unsuccessful and dissatisfied. Good capable staff leave.

3 Confusion builds up about priorities and objectives, leading to frustration across the organisation.

The Runaway Boss spiral

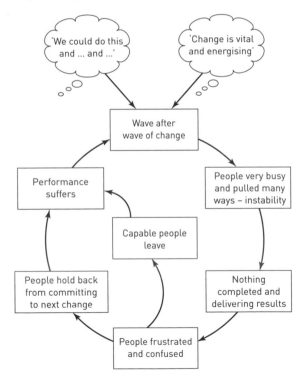

4 Staff become cynical and hold back their commitment and energy to any one change because they believe it will be superseded shortly by another.

If you try to fix the things that are broke and the things that aren't, all at the same time, then you leave yourself no capacity to deal with the unexpected.

DILEMMA 〉 DIAGNOSTIC 〉

Where do you tend to be?

Tortoise Boss diagnostic

Read the following and assess if they apply to you. If you would regularly agree with four or more of the statements, it's time to rethink whether you need to push your organisation to achieve more.

1 You are constantly holding back or losing people who seem to want change for change's sake.

2 You have had the same team, structure and approach for a long time.

3 You like to take time and think things through completely before committing yourself to a decision.

4 You always like to make sure that you have all the facts and evidence and an exact implementation plan before you go ahead with change.

5 You have been bypassed for leading new initiatives.

6 Your organisation/team constantly struggles to catch up with your competitors who just seem to move faster or further.

7 While you can see the benefits of change you usually feel the downside/risks outweigh the benefits and so don't start.

Runaway Boss diagnostic

· ·

Read the following and assess if they apply to you. If you would regularly agree with four or more of the statements, it's time to rethink how often you start change.

1 You are constantly surprised how long change takes.

2 You spend a lot more time explaining to people what you want than you think should be necessary.

3 People are strangely resistant to new ideas.

4 Your results are poorer than they should be, given the talent in the team.

5 People won't commit and drive change well.

6 You sometimes feel like you are the only source of new initiatives around.

7 You can see what's needed so clearly and don't know why others can't just get it.

This chapter describes how to get the balance right in terms of when to make change, enabling you to become a successful Driving Leader.

Balancing wisely

As leader, you are ultimately accountable for what your team or organisation delivers. Effective leaders apply high standards, aligned with the expectations of their customers or clients. Deciding what changes to make and when is a key leadership skill.

As one of the Group of Leaders[3] said *'The highest standard you get is the lowest standard you accept.'*

---

[3] The Group of Leaders refers to the 20 successful leaders interviewed for this book whose biographies can be found at the back of the book.

As for all the leadership dilemmas explored in this book, there are no perfect formulas. The art is to balance the benefits of the change in the widest sense, versus the cost of the change, again in the widest sense.

At certain times an organisation or team has to respond very fast to rapidly changing situations. In this context, it is important to be able to change quickly, possibly in several areas at a time. Overall direction needs to be very clear as decisions have to be faster and allow for adjustment as more information comes in. Clear consultation and communication is needed to keep checking whether the changes are still going to produce the outcomes expected in the changing environment – or whether further adjustment and possibly shedding of some initiatives is needed.

At other times and in different markets, organisations making large, very significant change decisions will have the time and opportunity to analyse and plan in depth before committing to one or another path. Timing is still an important element but may not be an immediate driver for action. In this case, clear consultation and communication is needed to make sure all relevant parties and information are accessed early enough to feed into the decision and to increase stakeholder buy-in.

As one leader put it, '*Good instinct, balanced with good thinking process, is most likely to give good decisions.*'

Productivity can be thought of as a cycle, as shown below. In a positive cycle, a good idea, well implemented, completed and learnt from, feeds into more successful ideas and actions. When this virtuous cycle is achieved, individuals and teams plan and execute activities well, leading to higher levels of energy, confidence and satisfaction.

The cycle of productivity

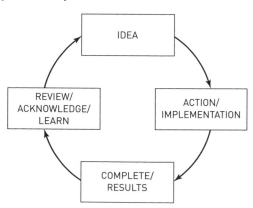

But often teams or individuals get stuck or avoid going round the full cycle. Runaway Bosses keep putting more and more ideas into the cycle without allowing things to be fully implemented, completed and reviewed. They therefore attract to them a lot of action-oriented people with few completer/finisher people and certainly no time or inclination for reviewing and learning.

The only time they are likely to review is when things have gone badly wrong. Then they risk over-reacting. As a result, fire-fighting increases and people lose sight of the objectives. Over time this

leads to poorer results, dissatisfaction and lower confidence.

Tortoise Bosses tend to get stuck focusing on planning and analysing risks and hold back too long on action-taking and post-action review. As a result they block creation of additional new ideas to improve the results yet further. Over time they risk the people they lead becoming too entrenched in their comfort zones and unwilling or resistant to change.

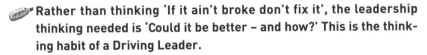 **Rather than thinking 'If it ain't broke don't fix it', the leadership thinking needed is 'Could it be better – and how?' This is the thinking habit of a Driving Leader.**

Good questions related to this mindset are:

> *Against what criteria should I decide what is better?*

> *What needs to change – for what and whose benefits?*

> *What is the change imperative?*

> *What are the enablers and blockers to change?*

> *On balance is change needed now/soon?*

> *What is our capability to change – now and later?*

When you operate from this perspective you become an effective Driving Leader because:

THE DRIVING LEADER

1 The reason for changing, *the 'Why'* is clearly linked to the purpose of the organisation and the group of people it serves and affects, creating buy-in from stakeholders.

2 The benefits can be articulated clearly: *the 'What you will get'.*

3 You take time to understand the impact and cost of change for the organisation , allowing you to focus on the most successful ways of changing: *the 'How'.*

4 By taking into account a realistic assessment of the organisation's ability to change you can set challenging but achievable goals and milestones: *the 'by When'.*

Working this way builds change confidence and capability, allowing you to look for further change faster in the future – or be better prepared to address dramatic changes to the organisation's position. It also prevents any complacency or people focusing on protecting their patch or comfort zone. Driving Leaders promote high performance and accountability.

An important point to consider is team balance. One of the best ways to compensate for either a Tortoise Boss or Runaway Boss tendency is to include a complementary person in the leadership team. But for this to be effective you need several things:

> self-awareness of your own change preferences and their impact;

> clarity about how others' skills and preferences contribute to better decisions;

> a willingness to listen and incorporate their approach as well as your own.

The role and value to a leader of self-awareness and seeking feedback is discussed further in Chapters 7 and 8.

The Driving Leader

One of the most important and potentially exciting areas of leadership is deciding that change is required and then leading that change successfully. The excitement comes from there being both opportunity and risk at stake. For many leaders this is where they get a real high from the job.

Driving Leaders demand and get the best from their organisations. Key components of their success are their ability to focus on the right changes at the right time and being able to mobilise people to make those changes. They are also capable of saying 'no' or 'not right now' to some change possibilities.

It is easier to *decide* things need to change when you are getting results and outcomes that are clearly falling short of customer, shareholder or staff expectations – or if the organisation faces significantly changed financial conditions. This is not to pretend that *implementing* change is necessarily easier to do in these circumstances. But, when it is clear to all concerned that change is necessary, the decision to make that change is easier.

The more difficult decisions are when:

> an organisation or group is working well right now and satisfying most existing demands; or

> the organisation or group is already making, or has just come through, one major change but more is required; or

> there are just so many changes needed it's difficult to know what to start with.

The factors Driving Leaders know to consider are:

1 Could things be better? What more is needed or desirable?

2 What needs to change?

3 What are the expected or desired benefits versus the cost and risks of change?

4 Do we have the capability to change now? If not, how will we develop it?

5 When is the right time?

Each of these is explored in more detail below.

How to assess the need to change

Leaders must be prepared to stand behind and be judged by the changes they decide to make. One of the most discomforting thoughts for those entering leadership roles is that they now have to put their head above the parapet and say what they believe is the right way forward. As one leader put it, '***You have to make a case and*** *stand by it.'* So it is vital to make a good assessment of the need to change – and when.

To answer the question 'Could things be better?', there are two key assessments to be made:

1 An honest appraisal of the current situation and performance.

2 A clear picture of what 'better' looks like, and from whose perspective.

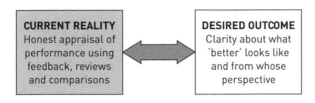

Making an honest appraisal of the current situation requires the leader, and/or leadership team, to stand back from day-to-day activities, let go of defensiveness and look and listen in a detached way. Important questions to ask are:

➤ *Is there a gap today in what we believe we provide and what our customers perceive we provide?*

➤ *Is there a gap between what it costs us to deliver and what it costs our competitors or other alternatives to our offering?*

➤ *Are there needs which are going unmet?*

➤ *Will there be a gap or unmet needs tomorrow?*

➤ *What changes have occurred or are occurring in terms of technology, processes, commercial terms, customer needs, organisational factors that make the way we operate less than fully effective?*

To answer these questions honestly, the leader needs to create feedback loops from customers, staff, market observers and, if appropriate, observation of competitors. As one leader said, '***Most of the time the organisation knows when things are wrong. It's up to the leader to ask and listen.***'

Effective leaders do not sit in an ivory tower within their headquarters. They devote time and energy to listening openly to their stakeholders and reflecting on the messages coming in. They have what many in the Group of Leaders referred to as 'a restless curiosity'.

They also ensure that not only they, but also others in the organisation, connect well with the external environment through avenues such as formal and informal networks, opinion surveys, trade journals and professional bodies.

It is not just about collecting facts here. It is about evaluating them and taking it on and selling it.

Most leaders are ambitious for their team or organisation. They are likely to have strong opinions. Formulating desired goals is relatively easy for them.

But, when asking the question 'Could it be better?', it is important to consider:

> *Better from whose perspective?*

> *Whose standards should I apply:*
>   – *the average recipient of the product/service;*
>   – *the most difficult or demanding customers;*
>   – *the most critical staff members;*
>   – *what our competitors offer;*
>   – *our own internal experts' opinion;*
>   – *our leadership team's views;*
>   – *company shareholders?*

All have legitimate views, but which ones should drive your decisions? The phrase 'ego-free listening' conveys an important message. To make good decisions about when and what to change, the leader and their supporting teams need to ensure they are not being driven solely by their own opinions.

A public affairs director in a large oil company once told me that every TV advert they put out had to go through the process of being approved by the executive team. Years of experience had shown that the more the executive team disliked or disapproved of the advert at a personal level, the more successful it

> was with the target audience of truck drivers. His job was to hold his nerve and remind them to do some 'ego-free listening' on each occasion!

Future trends are also important to consider. This could take the form of expert predictions, forecasts, scenario planning exercises, and related modelling and financial modelling processes. How much money and time should be invested in gathering such information will depend on the nature of the decision, the type of group or organisation you are, time-frames and the level of uncertainty. There is a wealth of strategic planning literature and advice available on this topic. For an excellent description on how to use scenario planning techniques, see Kees van der Heijden's *Scenarios: The Art of Strategic Conversation*.[4]

You've got to anticipate what's coming up, what are the challenges, what's the positioning we need.

Leaders tending towards the Tortoise Boss style are usually focusing too narrowly on getting the change decision and implementation just right rather than getting the direction, communication and timing clear. They can lose sight of how their slow decision making creates a potential communication vacuum, which leads to unnecessary rumour, anxiety and loss of momentum.

They may also have too strong a desire to be liked and fear they may upset people if they are constantly demanding higher performance. Either way, they need to deliberately seek greater external and internal challenge and be willing to trust their instincts on occasion. They also need to be prepared to step out of their own comfort zone and ask people around them to do the same.

Runaway Bosses have no problem assessing what needs to change. They need to give greater focus to gathering supporting data, listening to the feedback openly and creating effective prioritisation of the group's time and energies.

Tortoise Bosses can create procrastination by seeking too much data and not cutting through to the real information. Runaway

[4] Van der Heijden, K. (1996) *Scenarios: The Art of Strategic Conversation*, Chichester, England: John Wiley & Sons Ltd.

Bosses create confusion by relying on interesting snippets of information rather than balanced analysis and consultation.

The effective leader ensures that there is a process by which the multiple sources of data available are actually assimilated into useful information that is guiding decisions. This may be through vehicles such as strategic thinking processes, briefings to managers and leaders, and internal budgeting and challenge processes.[5]

It is all too easy for strong, effective teams or individual leaders to discount feedback, analysis and opinions that do not accord with their own view of the world or which contain unpalatable truths.

> Jane worked for a small consultancy that was growing fast. In order to plan well for the future, the CEO asked Jane and another senior manager to develop some scenarios of their future market and distil out the messages for the senior team.
>
> Jane and her colleague went through a scenario-planning exercise and were both surprised at some of the conclusions coming out of it. Their analysis showed that some contraction in the company's market was equally as likely as growth. They carefully talked through the logic of this conclusion with their directors. Everyone was in agreement that the logic was sound and there was a strong risk of a downturn soon. Cash flow could well be hit. Given the strong growth of the last few years, the message was unexpected and unpalatable.
>
> To Jane's surprise, some months later, the directors decided to recruit in 20% more new consultants and renew all the directors' cars. When the market turned down two months later, lack of cash flow hit the company hard. Two recent recruits had to be made redundant immediately, causing significant loss of morale all round. When Jane questioned what had happened between completing the future analysis and the decision to take on extra costs, the CEO admitted 'Logically, we understood the message, but I guess we just didn't want to hear it.'

[5] McKinsey Global Survey Results (December 2008) 'How Companies Make Good Decisions', *McKinsey Quarterly Review*.

When you lead a company you realise you have to push for not the best solution but the best solution everyone wants to implement.

In the end, a leader has to make a judgement about whether to change. That judgement is usually much easier to make if she is clear about the group cause (see Chapter 4), and has reliable, balanced information to consider.

Ultimately, two useful tests of a 'good' change are:

> Will it drive the group or organisation forward towards its purpose and shared goals?

> Will it increase flexibility for the future or constrain options?

How to assess what to change

If change is necessary, desirable, or both, the leader (or leadership team) needs to be clear what to change. In many cases that may be completely obvious. However, it is usually worth reflecting on what levers of change will give you the greatest effect for the lowest cost or impact.

The levers of change available may vary between different types of organisations and teams but the most common ones are shown in the diagram overleaf.

It is important at this stage to consider how things are linked and interdependent. For exam- 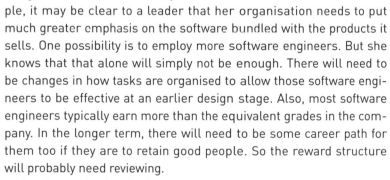 ple, it may be clear to a leader that her organisation needs to put much greater emphasis on the software bundled with the products it sells. One possibility is to employ more software engineers. But she knows that that alone will simply not be enough. There will need to be changes in how tasks are organised to allow those software engineers to be effective at an earlier design stage. Also, most software engineers typically earn more than the equivalent grades in the company. In the longer term, there will need to be some career path for them too if they are to retain good people. So the reward structure will probably need reviewing.

An alternative for the leader is to outsource the software design aspects of the process. But she knows that while this may seem less disruptive and simpler to manage, it will require a change in the organisation of the design process, may be slightly more expensive per man-hour and it may impact the existing team's morale if they feel loss of control or loss of professional challenge.

Often it is invaluable to get thoughts and inputs from managers and other experts when assessing what needs to change to get the desired outcome. Care needs to be given to make sure consultation will not cause unnecessary alarm amongst people, building resistance to the change before it is even agreed upon. Several of the Group of Leaders mentioned that consulting with and challenging people about how things could be done better was a vital part of building motivation and energy behind a change. Some excellent tools to help with this consultation and analysis can be found in Eddie Obeng's work.[6, 7]

Key levers for change

📌 **Understanding the levers of change you can use and how they may be linked allows you to fully assess the possible impact of different approaches before you make your decision.**

How to consider the benefits and costs of change

Being able to clearly articulate the benefits of the change may seem blindingly necessary, but can be forgotten once the initial desire for

[6] Obeng, E. (1994) *All Change! The Project Manager's Secret Handbook*, London: Pearson Education Ltd.
[7] Obeng, E. (2003) *Perfect Projects*, Beaconsfield, England: Pentacle Works, The Virtual Media Company.

change has taken hold. A key role the leader will play, if they go ahead with a change, is to communicate the benefits and the expected costs to stakeholders. Therefore it is very important that she understands these changes and how they may be viewed from different perspectives.

Most change does not come cost free. Even highly desirable change may require a person or a group to give up something, even if it is simply the comfort of existing routine.

> A major oil company planned to open a new office. A number of delays to the decision meant nothing happened for over four years. In the meantime, the company stopped spending any refurbishment money on the old offices and they got more crowded and run down. Staff complained about them all the time. When the new offices were finally ready they were very light, airy and relatively luxurious compared to the old. However, for the first few months the staff from the old, very scruffy office constantly complained how the new office was not as good as the old one and told fond stories of how good it was to work there. Complaining about their offices had become a familiar routine which they found hard to let go.

In some organisations or groups, formal cost/benefit analysis is the normal way in which change proposals are submitted for consideration and approval. This has the advantage of forcing people to think through what they expect to happen. Their assumptions and measurements of both benefits and costs have to be explicit.

Relying solely on cost/benefit analysis can lead to a spurious sense of comfort from its apparent accuracy. Firstly, people forget that the answer will only be as good as the quality of the underlying data and assumptions. Secondly, not all change decisions can be sensibly captured and analysed in this way, particularly if the costs or benefits are experienced on completely different measurement scales.

Thirdly, people can fail to include the benefits and costs of not changing, which may be a vital aspect of the decision.

Tortoise Bosses love the analysis and can get lost in making it precise rather than standing back to look at the real messages. Runaway Bosses are either moving too fast to do any analysis or do it very quickly without much care about the quality of the assumptions or logic.

There is a set of questions (much loved by coaches) which are useful in assessing costs and benefits, whether at a descriptive or fully quantified level. The questions are:

1 What will happen if I/we do this? (positive and negative)

2 What will not happen if I/we do this?

3 What will happen if I/we don't do this?

4 What will not happen if I/we don't do this?

These can be captured in a worksheet as follows:[8]

WHAT *WILL* HAPPEN IF I/WE CHANGE?	WHAT *WILL NOT* HAPPEN IF I/WE CHANGE?
Positive:	Positive:
Negative:	Negative:
WHAT *WILL* HAPPEN IF I/WE DO NOT CHANGE?	WHAT *WILL NOT* HAPPEN IF I/WE DO NOT CHANGE?
Positive:	Positive:
Negative:	Negative:

Experience of using these questions for a range of issues indicates that they are very effective for flushing out from decision makers their assumptions and concerns – whether expressed as hard or soft measures. It is important to include all the benefits in the 'positives' and all costs (including those that are perceived but may not be easily quantifiable) in the 'negatives'. This process is particularly useful in helping a group to have a dialogue about their expectations around a proposed change.

Sometimes, the question 'What will happen if we don't do this?' will simply produce answers that are the mirror image of 'What will

[8] Copies of the worksheet are available from the website, **www.badgeror doormat.com**.

happen if we do make the change?' However, on some occasions this does not prove to be the case. Often the act of considering the same question but effectively standing it on its head significantly widens the understanding of the real benefits and costs that need to be included.

For example, imagine a shopkeeper is deciding whether to hire another assistant. He knows if he goes ahead he will definitely incur additional costs but also that the assistant will free up his time, allowing him to investigate improving the shop's offering. His analysis shows that additional sales should cover the costs of the assistant. Normally that would be where he would complete his analysis and the decision would come down to assumptions about possible projected revenues versus known fixed costs.

However, when he goes through the questions on the worksheet he gets the following result.

WHAT *WILL* HAPPEN IF I HIRE THE ASSISTANT?	WHAT *WILL NOT* HAPPEN IF I HIRE THE ASSISTANT?
Positive: • I'll have more time to expand the business • I'll have more free time Negative: • I'll have additional costs of £X • I'll need to manage the assistant	Positive: • I'll stop having to do all the routine work Negative: • I'll have less direct contact with customers and possibly less understanding of their needs
WHAT *WILL* HAPPEN IF I DO NOT HIRE THE ASSISTANT?	WHAT *WILL NOT* HAPPEN IF I DO NOT HIRE THE ASSISTANT?
Positive: • I'll avoid the additional costs • I'll remain the main customer contact Negative: • I will cap/limit my business growth • I will have to do the routine work	Positive: • I won't have to change anything • I won't have the responsibility of employing another person Negative: • I won't learn to let someone else run parts of the business • I won't get any more free time

Once he has answered all four questions, the shopkeeper understands much more clearly that the key to making the decision lies in his long-term vision. If he eventually intends to run a chain of shops he will need a manager for the first shop. So it's not an assistant but a manager that he should look for as a sensible next step, providing the costs prove to be lower than the additional sales revenue he can generate. This is a first step in his business expansion.

Conversely, if the shopkeeper plans to be a profitable one-shop business focusing on good loyal customers, then the decision criteria are different. In this case he may weigh up whether it's an assistant he needs to allow him time to review the shop's offering, or whether he should bring in external expertise to do this and remain clearly the main point of contact with the customer.

In both cases, the shopkeeper still has to make assumptions and then a judgement. But he will alter the weight given to different costs and benefits depending on his goal for the future.

When considering benefits and costs, and before making the decision to change, it is always important to remember that one person's benefit may be another's cost. When considering any change, an effective leader needs to think it through from the perspective of each and every main stakeholder. This is greatly facilitated if the leader already has completed a stakeholder mapping exercise as described in Chapter 3.

At minimum, going through this process will enable the leader to articulate the change to each stakeholder in ways that have relevance to them. At best it will alert the leader to those stakeholders who are likely to have objections to the change and why. The leader can then include these objections in her decision-making process.

Tortoise Bosses need to balance their appreciation of the potential costs of change with a wider analysis of the potential benefits. Runaway Bosses need to make sure they consider the costs as other see them, and listen for objections as well as the benefits.

Weighing up the full range of benefits and costs allows the leader to answer more effectively the question – 'If change is needed, what's the right change for us?'

How to assess capability to change

Failure to consider the capability of the group, team or organisation to change is an underlying reason why change gets stuck or fails to produce the desired outcomes. Research by McKinsey & Company,[9] confirms that assessing the capability to change should be part of the

[9] McKinsey Global Survey Results (November 2008) 'Flaws in Strategic Decision Making', *McKinsey Quarterly Review*.

decision-making process about what to change and, in particular, when.

Some of the key factors affecting change capability are shown below. There may well be others which are particularly important in your specific context, but these are standard factors that can trip up the unwary. For more reading in this area see Michael Watkins's STaRS model[10] and the work of John Kotter.[11]

Factors affecting change capability

	Low	Medium	High	Critical
Imperative for and benefits from change clear to all				
Cohesive leadership group				
People resources available				
Energy level/enthusiasm				
Money resources available				
Change management experience versus size of change				
Clarity of risks				

Start by assessing – honestly – the group or organisation's capability for each factor. For example, if an organisation is regularly losing market share to a competitor, the imperative to change may be clear to all and would score a High. But falling revenues may hit the money available giving that a score of Low or Medium. If it is not clear what the risks are of making the change being considered then that would score Low. But if the organisation had successfully managed change of this size before that would score High.

It is also worth considering whether all these factors are critical for the particular decision being considered. For example, the change being proposed may not require significant money outlay, in which case monetary resources are not important in the assessment.

[10] Watkins, M. (2003) *The First 90 Days: Critical Success Strategies for New Leaders at all Levels*, Boston: Harvard Business School Publishing.
[11] Kotter, J.P. (January 2007) 'Leading Change: Why Transformation Efforts Fail', *Harvard Business Review*.

If the leader's assessment of the organisation's change capability is as shown in the grid below, she knows that lack of clarity about the risks is the weakest area. This may be sufficiently important to make her hold off the decision to implement the proposed change until she can increase clarity.

	Low	Medium	High	Critical
Imperative for and benefits from change clear to all			✓	Yes
Cohesive leadership group		✓——→		Yes
People resources available			✓	Yes
Energy level/enthusiasm		✓——→		Yes
Money resources available	✓			No
Change management experience versus size of change			✓	Yes
Clarity of risks	✓———————→			Yes

Alternatively, she could decide there is sufficient capability and she needs to go ahead to meet some aspect of good timing in the market. She knows from this analysis that one of the first things the team must do in implementation is to understand the risks and how to manage them better. She also knows she has to take actions to increase the cohesiveness of her leadership team and the levels of energy and readiness in the staff.

Runaway Bosses tend to either miss out consideration of change capability or skip vital areas. They need to hold their own enthusiasm in check and take a critical look at the current change capability in the organisation they lead. Ideally, they will start by consulting and listening to their senior managers' views before initiating further change.

Interestingly, some Tortoise Bosses may also miss out good analysis of change capability as they get stuck going round cost/benefit calculations that do not give them clear results. In this case, bringing in a review of change capability may enable them to broaden their thinking and refocus them on the direction they want to go.

Alternatively, Tortoise Bosses may be over-worried about change capability and/or underestimating what their people are capable of

achieving. They need to be bolder in demanding more and taking actions that may stress the organisation for periods of time. It is important to remember that although it may be stressful, most people's 'career highs' are born from achieving challenging change.

Assessing people's energy and enthusiasm for change can be difficult. It may be a popular change which everyone thinks is timely or overdue and/or may give personal benefits. In this case energy will naturally be higher than for a change that requires reducing the workforce or significantly changing the way people work.

Also, where an organisation has successfully implemented change in the past and it expanded people's opportunities and performance, then there will clearly be an appetite for change. However, if the organisation has a history of badly implemented and relatively unsuccessful change, or is in the middle of very significant change right now, energy and enthusiasm for more will be lower.

In assessing the likely energy, it can be useful to have a mental model of the various stages people go through during change. A simple but effective model is shown below.

The DREC change model

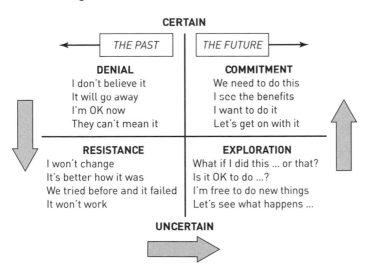

The first reaction to news of change is **D**enial. Even very positive news, like winning the lottery, is initially greeted with phrases like 'I can't believe it!' In organisations it may take the form of 'It'll not happen. You'll see.'

The next stage is **R**esistance. For our lottery winner this may be expressed as 'I won't let it change me.' In organisations it can be explicit resistance in the form of 'I know we are supposed to do it the new way but I think the old way was better so I'll keep doing that.' Alternatively, more covert forms of resistance may occur in the form of subtle undermining and ambiguous communication. The key thing about people in this stage is they are still focused on how it was in the past and why that needs to be retained.

The third stage is **E**xploration. Now the person has accepted the possibility of change and they start exploring what it could mean for them. A lottery winner might say things like 'Well, I suppose I could have a new car, and a holiday and . . . and . . .' Some lottery winners famously get stuck in this stage and spend all their money very quickly. In organisations this exploration takes the form of lots of questions, often pushing pre-existing boundaries. Examples are, 'So, after the change will we all get . . .?' and 'There might be an opportunity for me to do . . .' In this stage people are looking at the possibilities with little sense of responsibility for the outcomes.

The fourth and final stage is **C**ommitment. Here people have accepted the change, can see the new possibilities, positive and negative, and take responsibility for making the change happen successfully. In the case of our lottery winner they might say 'I'm going to talk this through with an adviser to make sure I get the best use of the money.' In organisations, people in Commitment take on responsibilities for aspects of the change and are willing to communicate to others the need for the change and what the benefits will be.

Leaders are there to provide the fertiliser, the message about change, but people have to recognise the need to change themselves.

Individuals move through these stages at very different rates depending on:

> the nature of the change;

> where others in the group are; and

> their own ability to embrace change.

Also, progress is not linear. Some falling back to earlier stages occurs as difficulties or doubts are encountered.

For a leader deciding whether to make a change, it is important to consider:

> where the bulk of their group is currently in respect of previous change; and

> the group's previous pace of change.

If the majority of the group are still in Resistance or even Denial in respect of a previous change, any further change may encounter significant resistance too – especially if it appears to be linked. While this may not be a valid reason to avoid making a further change, the leader needs to consider whether it is sufficient reason to hold off until potential energy and enthusiasm can be increased again. If the majority of people are in Commitment or still Exploring, additional change is more likely to be successfully assimilated.

Just as some individuals may accept certain changes faster than others, it is also true that some people and some groups will embrace change much faster than others. Going through change is something that people are usually better at if they do it more regularly – up until the point where overuse leads to change fatigue. In assessing change capability, an effective Driving Leader needs to consider the group's inherent change readiness as well as its level of change 'fitness'.

How to assess when to change

The key message here is: Change when you are in the strongest position to change successfully. As one of the Group of Leaders put it, 'Start change when you are in a strong position and you are in control because if you leave it too late you may be forced to change from a weak starting point.'

Clearly, if a change is critical to the business and external forces making the change imperative are very strong, then now may be the only option. But there are other times when it is positive and desirable to change. A good question to ask is: *Will starting a change later improve or diminish the factors affecting our capability to change i.e.:*

> *the visibility of the imperative to change;*

> *the cohesiveness and strength of the leadership team;*

> *the people resources available;*

> *the energy or enthusiasm levels;*
> *the financial resources;*
> *the change management capability;*
> *our clarity about the risks; and*
> *other context-specific factors?*

Simon was the newly appointed leader of IT programme delivery in a company that had a big goal to go from £300m revenue to £900m in the next five years. IT was a crucial enabler of their service and the IT division had recently been reorganised to support this growth ambition.

It was clear to Simon that he needed to reorganise to get his whole area to focus and respond better to the business's needs. He reviewed the factors that would affect the likely success of a change and decided to delay his reorganisation for a number of reasons.

> The executive team was about to launch a roadshow to communicate the big goals clearly and the message that things would need to change to deliver this – Simon knew this would increase the visible imperative for change for his managers.

> People had just come through the reorganisation at Simon's level and above and the cohesiveness of this leadership team would probably be higher when people had settled fully into their new positions.

> Simon wanted a chance to assess people in their current situation to understand their capabilities and style.

> He wanted time to build good relationships with his stakeholder colleagues in the rest of the business to make sure his planned change would best match their requirements.

> Some big projects would be completed within a few months so by delaying the reorganisation he could avoid disrupting these at a critical stage and also would have more available manpower and energy during the change.

> By being able to articulate his thinking clearly and show it was well grounded in both the business goals and the current context, Simon was able to get his senior team's approval for his plan.

It may be a balancing act, but if making the change at a later time improves the overall chances of success, then a Driving Leader needs to have the ability and patience to wait.

Runaway Bosses need to develop their ability to look at all the factors that will affect the success of the change and learn to hold off, if necessary, until the timing is right. Tortoise Bosses need to learn to look around the corner at what may be coming towards their organisation and start to make change early rather than missing the window of opportunity and having to play catch-up.

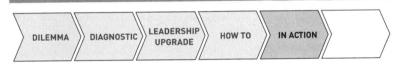

DILEMMA 〉 DIAGNOSTIC 〉 LEADERSHIP UPGRADE 〉 HOW TO 〉 IN ACTION 〉

The Driving Leader in action

John was the MD of a large shipping and delivery company. He had just led the company through a major change programme to meet growing customer demand for guaranteed overnight delivery. The changes had not always been easy, and the company had to think and work very hard to deliver on the new promises. But now the service was available and working and the company was the leader in the market.

One day, John heard his customer services people complaining about one particular customer: 'He's just unreasonable. Even with the overnight service he's still not happy. He says he wants the same day delivery. I don't know how he thinks we are going to do that!'

John was intrigued. So he asked this customer if he could visit him. When they met John asked him what it was that he wanted. The customer replied, 'I need to get my packages the 250 or more miles from your depots to my offices in Devon the same day my customer hands the package to you. Overnight just won't work.'

John listened some more, and then asked a very important question: 'How do you see us doing that?'

'Well,' the customer replied somewhat testily, 'If I had a car at your depot I'd get someone to stick it in the car and drive it to me!'

'And how do I get the driver there and back in one day – assuming you don't want to incur the cost of two man-days' time and expenses to stay over?' asked John.

'Ah, if that's your problem,' said the customer, 'I could meet you halfway. It would still be better for me than one of my guys driving all the way.'

John was surprised at the simplicity and clarity of this response. Recovering quickly, he asked, 'If I could organise a within-day service what would you be prepared to pay for it?' The customer had a long think about this and named his price. John thanked him very much for taking the time to talk to him and said he would let him know as soon as he had a same-day service available.

Then John sat and thought about his dilemma. He knew that to ask his team to start afresh and design a cost-effective same-day delivery service would be like asking them to get back up on a tightrope having just successfully climbed off the tightrope of the last change. He could just leave them a bit longer enjoying the satisfaction of knowing they had cracked what had been seen as a massive change and the glory of being market leaders. To ask for more radical innovation now could demotivate them and possibly even reduce the effectiveness with which the new services were being rolled out.

On the other hand, after this customer conversation, John believed they could be the first to offer a unique, viable and valuable service to their customers. Potentially, there was a big business prize available. They didn't need to wait for their competitors to be breathing down their necks to take the next leap.

Despite knowing that he would be seen as unreasonable and possibly considered crazy, John put the challenge to his senior team. Their reaction was as predicted. For a while they told him it could not be done and there was no evidence that many people wanted the same-day service.

John persisted. He acknowledged the customer's proposed solution was not the right one but other solutions might exist if they just thought about it differently. He invited the marketing department to at least test what the demand might be. He also pointed out the strong capability to innovate and change which the company had just demonstrated it had. He talked about the satisfaction of leaving their competition way behind in service capability. Slowly he convinced a number of other people it was worth seriously considering.

John knew that once he had some key people willing to embrace the challenge (even if it was the challenge to prove him wrong!), there was a good possibility of creating the new service – capturing a valuable, unique market opportunity. Some months later John was delighted to launch a same-day express delivery service.

DILEMMA 〉 DIAGNOSTIC 〉 LEADERSHIP UPGRADE 〉 HOW TO 〉 IN ACTION 〉 **SUMMARY**

SUMMARY OF KEY POINTS

1 Fully effective leaders initiate the right changes at the right time to deliver successfully their organisation's purpose and goals.

2 The leadership thinking that supports successful Driving Leaders is: 'Could it be better and how?'

3 Standing back and assessing from several viewpoints your change options and their impact will allow you to make more successful changes.

4 Gathering and listening to feedback from outside and inside the organisation is vital to enable you to understand what is or may become needed.

5 It is vital to ensure that the gathered feedback and analysis is fully acknowledged and assimilated into useful information that guides your decisions.

6 Understanding the levers of change you can use and how they may be linked allows you to fully assess the possible impact of different approaches.

7 Understanding all the expected benefits and costs and how different people see them allows you to make sure the most important alternatives are given priority.

▶

8 Assessing the organisation or group's capability to change is an important factor when deciding what and when to change as it will greatly affect the likely success of different options.

9 If one or several aspects of change capability is critically low, it is important to consider ways to increase that capability before starting.

10 Make change when you are in the strongest position to change successfully – that could be now or at a future date.

Coaching questions

Initiating the right changes at the right time for the success of the group or organisation is a vital leadership task. This section pulls together the powerful questions in the chapter plus other questions to help you do this effectively.

Suggestions on how best to use these coaching questions can be found in the coaching questions section of Chapter 2.

Deciding the change imperative

> *What is the change imperative?*

> *Is there a gap today in what we believe we provide and what our customers perceive we provide?*

> *Is there a gap between what it costs us to deliver and what it costs our competitors or other alternatives to our offering?*

> *Are there needs which are going unmet?*

> *Will there be a gap or unmet needs tomorrow?*

> *What changes have occurred or are occurring in terms of technology, processes, commercial terms, customer needs, organisational factors that make the way we operate less than fully effective?*

> *Is there an opportunity window?*

Assessing what to change

➤ Is the desired outcome or goal clear?

➤ What levers of change do I have? Which might be most effective?

➤ What issues and factors might be linked or interdependent?

➤ Who would give me valuable insights into what will be needed?

Assessing if it is a 'good' change

➤ Whose criteria should I apply to decide 'good':
  - the average recipient of the product/service;
  - the most difficult or demanding customers;
  - the most critical staff members;
  - what our competitors offer;
  - our own internal experts' opinion;
  - our leadership team's views;
  - our shareholders?

➤ Will it drive the group or organisation forward towards its purpose and shared goals?

➤ Will it increase flexibility for the future or constrain options?

➤ What will happen if I/we do this? (positive and negative)

➤ What will not happen if I/we do this?

➤ What will happen if I/we don't do this?

➤ What will not happen if I/we don't do this?

➤ How will the change impact on different stakeholders?

Assessing capability to change

➤ How clear, strong and visible is the imperative to change?

➤ How cohesive is the leadership team?

➤ Are there enough people to handle the extra load of making this change? If not, how could we get more people resources?

➤ How much energy and enthusiasm will there be for making this change?

➤ Is the group change-ready, focused elsewhere or overloaded?

➤ Will the change require financial input and if so will the money be available?

➤ What change management experience do we have or can we use?

➤ How clear are the risks?

➤ What other enablers and blockers to change can people see?

Assessing when to change

➤ Will starting later improve or diminish the factors affecting our capability to make this change?

Chapter 7

The leadership jigsaw – common principles used by successful leaders

- Leadership themes (p. 162)
- Vision, passion and ambition (p. 163)
- Values and connecting with people (p. 168)
- Personal enablers: self-management and self-renewal (p. 174)
- Conclusions (p. 184)

Leadership themes

What makes effective leadership? Well, as Chapters 2 to 6 have shown, one aspect is the ability to resolve dilemmas and continually match your leadership behaviours to those needed for different contexts. But compelling leadership has more to it than that.

In the course of researching this book I interviewed 20 successful leaders in a wide range of different companies, sectors and institutions.[1] We talked about principles they used to guide them in making effective decisions. I was very struck by the commonality of messages I heard and realised there was something fundamental being said about successful leadership. You will find these fundamentals in this chapter.

The leaders' messages came through in both:

> the principles they explicitly talked about; and

> the stories they told about putting these into practice.

Some of the leaders had very consciously considered and developed their leadership style and behaviours. Others told me, 'I've simply just noticed what did and didn't work for me over the years.' What they all have in common is a self-awareness about how they operate as a leader and an openness to feedback on their leadership style. They have strong leadership presence – they are very present when they interact with people.

In his book *Good to Great*[2] Jim Collins talks about the positive and inspiring impact that researching and meeting level 5 leaders had on him and his researchers. Collins defines these leaders as people who 'build enduring greatness through a paradoxical blend of personal humility and professional will.' While the leaders I interviewed for this book may be too modest to put themselves forward as level 5 leaders, I was deeply aware that they display this same blend of enormous ambition and drive for their organisation's success, combined with great self-awareness of their own strengths and vulnerabilities.

---

[1] Short biographies of these leaders, referred to as the Group of Leaders, can be found at the back of the book.

[2] Collins, J. (2001) *Good to Great: Why some companies make the leap . . . and others don't*, London: Random House Business Books.

Many of the Group of Leaders were pleased to contribute to this practical leadership book 'to help others avoid having to learn by making the same mistakes as I've made.' Hence I have drawn together their thoughts in the form of insights to consider when reviewing your own leadership style.

These 'Lessons from the Leaders' are grouped into three specific themes:

1 Vision, passion and ambition.

2 Values and connecting with people.

3 Personal enablers: self-management and self-renewal.

These principles will be invaluable to you in understanding how to increase the effectiveness of your leadership style. When implemented, they will make you more successful in dealing with the inevitable pressures and challenges of a leadership role.

Vision, passion and ambition

'Begin with the end in mind' is one of Stephen Covey's *Seven Habits of Highly Effective People*.[3] Covey points out that everything is created twice: once in the mind's eye and once in reality. He states 'leadership deals with the top line: what are the things I /we want to accomplish?' The concept of using your mind's eye to focus and direct your thoughts is elegantly expanded in George Kohlrieser's *Hostage at the Table*[4] in which he says 'the mind's eye makes it possible to achieve just about anything we want – the important element is to focus on the positive outcome.'

All 20 of the Group of Leaders spoke of the need to be clear about what you want, where you are going and why. As shown in the diagram overleaf, the benefits from clarity of vision are:

> You create and communicate a sense of common purpose and direction, making people's tasks more meaningful, satisfying and therefore motivating.

[3] Covey, S.R. (1989) *Seven Habits of Highly Effective People*, London: Simon and Schuster Ltd.
[4] Kohlrieser, G. (2006) *Hostage at the Table*, San Francisco: Jossey-Bass.

➤ Your decision making is faster and more effective as it is aligned to where you want to be in the future.

➤ Prioritising your own and other people's focus and energy is easier.

➤ Delegation is more successful as people understand the outcome they are moving towards.

➤ You attract followers with the right ambitions and skills to fulfil your common purpose.

➤ You have greater resilience and ability to take advantage of unexpected external events and demands without losing your direction and momentum.

When they are absent, you:
- send mixed messages about what is wanted
- under-challenge the team to produce results
- slip into daily fire-fighting as your main focus
- create conflicting objectives for people and subsequent conflict
- struggle to make decisions quickly
- fail to attract other ambitious and passionate deliverers
- get pushed off course by obstacles and setbacks

VISION PASSION AMBITION

When they are present, you:
- communicate common purpose and direction
- make people's tasks more meaningful, satisfying and motivating
- make effective decisions today aligned to where you want to be in the future
- prioritise easily your own and others' focus and energy
- delegate successfully as people understand the outcomes wanted
- attract followers with the right ambitions and skills
- have greater resilience to overcome unexpected events

Interestingly, in *Built to Last*[5] Collins and Porras show their findings that stock returns were positively correlated with constancy of purpose and values.

Whether you call it vision, mission, cause or goal, it needs to be compelling and meaningful to your followers. It needs to relate to the common purpose you collectively serve. When that is in place it drives people forward to take action and 'step up' to the challenge.

That purpose will vary enormously between organisations and groups and will often be implicitly understood rather than explicitly stated. One of the leader's tasks is to encapsulate that purpose

[5] Collins J. and Porras, J. (1994) *Built to Last*, New York: HarperCollins.

within a picture of the future that people want to work towards. The vision should describe a future where that purpose is being fulfilled in a positive and exciting way for people delivering the results and the people receiving the product and/or service. Robert Dilts describes this as 'creating a world to which people want to belong'.[6]

One important point is to understand the difference between the strategy of someone who is investing in the enterprise versus the strategy of the enterprise itself. It is highly likely that the investor's strategy is to make a  desired financial return on their money. They will want to drive the enterprise to success in terms of profit and shareholder value as that would be a fair reflection of the purpose and vision for their organisation.

However, outside financial institutions or functions, most people do not answer the question 'What do you do?' or 'What does your organisation do?' with 'We make a y% return on capital.' Most people's answers will be about the *activities their organisation does and for whom*. This is their reality. Shareholders invest in teams and enterprises with a compelling strategy – that's why they have put their money in. Effective leaders understand that the purpose, vision and mission of their group need to be expressed in ways that have meaning and are motivational for themselves, their followers and their financial backers. This can take time to get right but the rewards for doing so are multiple and are felt right across the group or organisation.

Vision, passion and ambition

· ·

Leaders' messages

The higher up the organisation you get the more you realise the people who are successful have that clarity of vision of what they are about and why they are doing it coupled with a passion to get it done.

Dave Mutton, Electralink Ltd

▶

[6] Dilts, R. (1996) *Visionary Leadership Skills*, California: Meta Publications.

The value of vision is to drive the thinking on what you need to do right now to make it happen.

David Vaughan, Wragge & Co

There's a big difference between having the vision/purpose/ values on paper and having them enter into the DNA of the organisation. That throws up for me the level of commitment – to what extent am I personally committed such that I will risk failure to achieve this?

Dorothy Nesbit, Learning for Life (Consulting) Ltd

It's got to be something people really connect to at a personal level and internalise. So you've got to make that vision seem very personal and create that passion about it.

Michael McNicholas, ESB International

To me, that is one of the key points in doing something significant, something extraordinary. It is actually the point at which you commit yourself personally as leader and say 'look this is going to happen' – and people see no uncertainty in your eyes.

John Shine, ESB

You have to have character in the business and it sort of comes from the leader and goes all the way down. It's his views in life – very fundamental. It filters and permeates throughout the whole business in every type of thing you do.

Mike Clare, Dreams plc

Stepping up and accepting accountability to set the organisation's direction comes with risk. Many refer to it as having to put your head above the parapet and risk being shot at. It takes courage to do so.

That courage is greatly enhanced when we are passionate about something and develop an inner conviction it is the right thing to do. Many of the

Group of Leaders talked about having or creating personal passion and energy to deliver the vision. That passion and energy is often most effectively expressed when aligned with strong ambition for the success of the organisation or group as a whole. This echoes Jim Collins's advice that success comes from doing what you are passionate about.

Creating vision, passion and energy is not limited to a few gifted communicators. It starts with creating a high level of *internal commitment* and passion to a goal. Some of the Group of Leaders talked about the process of consultation, reflection and evaluation they go through before committing themselves and others to big goals. They understand the power that strong internal certainty brings when they go out to say 'It is possible – and we are going to do it.' Followers do not always 'buy in' to the vision immediately. A leader needs to take time to communicate it and adapt or develop it further to build a shared picture of the future.

People are attracted to leaders who communicate, even radiate, confidence and certainty of purpose. Simplicity is an important factor in articulating the message.

Communication comes through not just what you say but also what you do. In particular, followers watch:

> what you show interest in and spend time on;
> the team that you champion;
> the resources that are made available.

When your actions are aligned to your communications you produce a compelling sense of direction and commitment for others. Your example helps your followers to align themselves and so the effects of your behaviours ripple positively down the organisation.

If you want to assess your level of clarity about your vision, passion and ambition, some good questions to ask are:

> *Can you state where you want to go in one, or at most two, simple sentences?*
> *Are you personally excited and challenged by the vision and future goal?*
> *Is it big enough a goal to stretch the talents of your team and make a real difference – but not so big no one takes it seriously?*

> *When you state it out loud, do you feel both positive and sure it is worthwhile?*

> *When you consider the alternative ways you could use the time and resources you will use in achieving this vision, will it be worth it?*

> *When others in your group or team hear the vision, does it make sense to them and are they energised to accept the challenge?*

> *Has creating the vision made you clearer about what are the right choices and decisions to make when faced with different attractive possibilities?*

The key messages about vision, passion and ambition

1 Commit to a vision and purpose that is compelling, meaningful and motivating for you and the group.
2 Be sure you have internal energy and passion for it.
3 Articulate it in a clear, simple way through what you think, say and do.

Values and connecting with people

One vital leadership lesson is 'It's all about the people piece'. The Group of Leaders all agreed you have to be interested in the people dynamic. This may be something you are naturally interested in or it may be something you have to develop – but it's another fundamental piece of the leadership jigsaw.

Liking the 'people piece' should not be confused with liking people. This is not about winning a popularity contest. It is about being curious and able to engage with all different types of people to achieve things for and with the group you lead. This skill of reading and connecting with people is part of the emotional intelligence that is required for effective leadership today.

Another vital aspect of the 'people piece' is choosing the right team for the right roles. It's more than getting very capable individuals engaged. You have to consider the dynamics of the team as a whole – how they will interact with each other, how their respective strengths will balance out each

others' and your own weaker areas. This requires honesty and respect of each other's unique abilities (see Chapter 5 for more on this topic). These essential values are discussed below.

> *The longer you do it, the more you realise that leadership is not formulaic, it's all about people. It's a scary fact.*
>
> **Mark Dearnley, Cable & Wireless plc**
>
> *An effective leader is able to recognise the unique potential in individuals and has a clear sense of how to unleash it within teams.*
>
> **Chong-Meng Tan, Shell Eastern Petroleum (Pte) Ltd**
>
> *The real art of being the leader of a strong team is to get the strong players to work together rather than in conflict. Leadership teams are far more powerful than individuals. If you create a climate where those powerful people can work together, you create a very powerful force.*
>
> **Chris Floyd, Rolls-Royce plc**

One of the key ways in which you connect with people is through the values you demonstrate and support. Values form an integral part of the culture of any group. Often they are part of the glue binding a group together.

Clearly, groups will differ in both their values and the accepted behaviours that express those values. However, three were mentioned by all the leaders interviewed: *respect*, *honesty* and *integrity*. These are seen as non-negotiable for effective leadership.

Respect, honesty and integrity

Treating everyone with respect is an essential mindset for an effective leader. Respectful leadership behaviours that the Group of Leaders mentioned include:

- ➤ accepting that others will have different values and priorities and respecting their different choices;
- ➤ addressing people in ways that make them feel comfortable and listened to;
- ➤ being welcoming and engaging and thanking people for talking/presenting to you even if you do not agree with them;
- ➤ acknowledging the work others have put in for you;
- ➤ taking time to understand and empathise with the needs of the other rather than simply imposing your own needs;
- ➤ being clear that someone is 'OK' as a person but their skills and talents may just not fit here in this group at this point in time.

One facet of leadership is accepting that you cannot please all the people all the time. You may set out your direction and the opportunities as you see them, but you respect individuals whose choices may be governed by different priorities.

Building and maintaining a very respectful mindset is a valuable habit effective leaders reinforce for themselves and others.

Respect, honesty and integrity

Leaders' messages

'Everybody is entitled to respect. They have their own values and priorities – these are for them to choose, and you should respect their freedom to choose. In a fluid society, where people can make their own choices, you can address them in ways that make them comfortable and able to give of their best in return.

Roger Mountford, CAA

Reflecting on my expectations of my leader I want to know what the guy stands for. I want to be sure there is no hidden agenda, that this is transparent, that he shares openly what he wants to achieve and I want to be reasonably sure that he keeps his part of the contract.'

Josef Waltl, Shell International Petroleum Company Ltd

Always giving the facts and not tricking people is very important and would be a guiding rule.

Spiro Santoni, RBS

I'm sure I could have got from where I was to where I needed to be by a little bit of fancy footwork, telling the half truth and so on but I would know I have done that. I would look in the mirror and think I don't really respect you for how you did that. So for me, I think respecting the way I have done something is important not just was the outcome right.

Pamela Taylor, Water UK

In good leadership honesty is coupled with a kind of morality.

Major General John Chester

Being transparent, honest and acting with integrity are vital behaviours for sustainable, effective leadership. All the leaders interviewed mentioned these as key values – essential ingredients for building respect and effective communication with others. When you step away from these values you run the risk of not only losing the trust and respect of others but also losing your own anchor and guiding foundation.

Honesty and integrity in this sense do not necessarily mean:

> hurting people unnecessarily with, for example, unconstructive feedback; or

> saying things before they need to be said and creating confusion in those around you.

If absent, can lead to:
- causing unnecessary and unintended offence
- losing ideas from people whose talents are different
- low influence as your words are distrusted or discounted
- imposing your own needs and views on others creating demotivation or resistance
- tripping yourself up when you can't remember who told you what to do
- building false expectations and confusion around you
- avoiding dealing with difficult people or situations

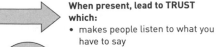

RESPECT HONESTY INTEGRITY

When present, lead to TRUST which:
- makes people listen to what you have to say
- makes people prepared to go the extra mile for you/the group
- allows effective two-way feedback and open dialogue
- allows people to accept your decisions – positive and negative
- allows effecive delegation and communication of results
- attracts followers to come through change with you

It does mean being honest with yourself and others about the situation you/they are in, what you want from them, the options they have, and reasons behind decisions. Consistently behaving this way builds respect and trust for what you say.

Trust

Trust has been called the greatest of qualities. Leaders who operate with respect, honesty and integrity build a vital ingredient – trust. Trust within the leader–follower relationship gives many benefits including:

> People listen and are open-minded about what you have to say.

> Effective two-way feedback happens, allowing issues to be addressed openly and learning to be faster.

> People are willing to risk challenging you, the leader, and/or put forward new, potentially risky ideas.

> People want to go the extra mile to make things happen for you or the group.

> Effective delegation happens as you can hand over responsibility knowing the individual can be trusted to deliver and keep you adequately informed.

> People are willing to follow you through change when they fundamentally don't like change.

Trust is also vital within the wider group of stakeholders that leaders need to engage with. For example, directors of public companies who can build trust amongst the city analysts become more attractive to investors and thereby potentially increase the value of their organisation.

Trust

Leaders' messages

Most people don't like change. If you are going to make a big shift, you have to sell that they can trust you and you have to, through your relationships with them, let them know you can be trusted and you will deliver.

Cathy Gronquist, Morgan Stanley

You appear to transact with companies, but actually you don't – you transact with individuals. You're actually doing deals with people, on behalf of organisations . . . you can write a 1000-page contract – it means very little compared to what you can achieve with a great relationship.

Mark Dearnley, Cable & Wireless plc

The shadow of the leader is such that whatever we say, when the chips are down, it is the way we behave that matters.

John Wybrew, Chairman, British Energy Association

If you want to assess your level of connection with people through respect, honesty and integrity some good questions to ask are:

> *Do you flex your own behaviours and style to make other people more comfortable or feel positive about interacting with you?*

> *Do you think through others' needs and perspectives while still being clear about your own position?*

> *What do you think of people who hold different views from you – interesting, misguided or not worth spending time with?*

> *Are you open and clear about your agenda or would people perceive you as regularly having hidden agendas?*

> *How much thinking time do you devote to solving issues around products, services and processes versus solving issues around power and politics or the culture of the organisation?*

> *How well do you deal with difficult people questions or difficult situations – engage with them openly or duck them in the hope they will go away, usually to find they only got worse?*

> *Do people often come to you for honest feedback and explanation?*

Of course your level of honesty about yourself will affect your answers to these questions!

The key messages about values and connecting with people

1 Develop an interest and focus on people and the people dynamics.

2 Ensure you are living the values of respect, honesty and integrity.

3 Trust is built by living and expressing those values continuously.

4 People will connect well with you and your message when you can build trust.

Personal enablers: self-management and self-renewal

Six key personal enablers around self-management and self-renewal were discussed regularly by the Group of Leaders:

1 Self-awareness.

2 Self-reliance.

3 Creating reflective time.

4 Managing your energy.

5 Decisiveness.

6 Continued learning and development.

The primary factors in self-management are self-awareness, self-reliance and decisiveness. They give you the ability to manage your own responses so you can create the impact and message you want. Using reflective time, managing your energy and continued learning allow you, as a leader, to replenish your own sense of vision, passion and commitment. They also allow you to renew the necessary stamina and resilience to keep listening for feedback and stretching yourself and others.

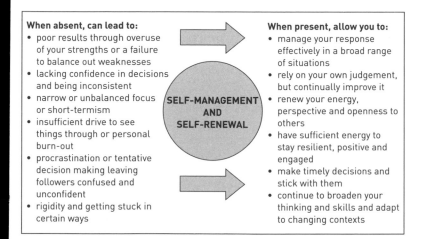

When absent, can lead to:	When present, allow you to:
• poor results through overuse of your strengths or a failure to balance out weaknesses	• manage your response effectively in a broad range of situations
• lacking confidence in decisions and being inconsistent	• rely on your own judgement, but continually improve it
• narrow or unbalanced focus or short-termism	• renew your energy, perspective and openness to others
• insufficient drive to see things through or personal burn-out	• have sufficient energy to stay resilient, positive and engaged
• procrastination or tentative decision making leaving followers confused and unconfident	• make timely decisions and stick with them
• rigidity and getting stuck in certain ways	• continue to broaden your thinking and skills and adapt to changing contexts

Centre circle of figure: **SELF-MANAGEMENT AND SELF-RENEWAL**

Self-awareness

No leader is perfect. Self-awareness enables you to ensure you use your own strengths to full advantage.[7] You can then compensate by either paying more attention to your less preferred areas or building a team around you that balances your strengths.

[7] Nomura, C. and Waller, J. (1995–2006) *Discover Your Unique Abilities*, Ontario: The Strategic Coach Inc.

Confident self-awareness is one of the vital ingredients of emotionally intelligent leadership. Being able to read and understand your own responses and behaviours is one part of the equation. Self-confidence allows you to do this accurately without creating disabling self-doubt.

With this self-knowledge you can learn to manage your response in ways that will be more productive for you and/or others. By increasing your flexibility of response you increase your ability to operate effectively when faced with a broad set of situations and challenges.

One aspect of self-awareness several leaders mentioned is the trap of trying to lead in all types of situations. While some truly adept people can lead in most situations, it was widely acknowledged that most good leaders have strengths that suit particular contexts and not others. Knowing what your leadership style is and playing to its strengths is very important. Acknowledging when it is no longer a good fit for a leadership role in a changed context is equally important.

Self-awareness

Leaders' messages

I think self–awareness is about being critical about yourself, challenging yourself. There is not a single day I can remember where in the evening I was completely satisfied. There is always something that I was thinking 'I should have done that' or 'I shouldn't have done that'. This is not a conscious sitting down and thinking – it's just a natural thing.

Josef Waltl, Shell International Petroleum Company Ltd

The leader must be completely self-aware or as much as possible. A leader can also change so you can shape your leadership signature.

Chong-Meng Tan, Shell Eastern Petroleum (Pte) Ltd

Self-reliance

In his book *Emotional Capitalists*[8] Martyn Newman tells us:

'From the studies of high performing leaders the first and most interesting feature in the profile of successful entrepreneurs was their high score on the emotional competency of self-reliance. This is perhaps not surprising – after all how could you run an organisation without independence of mind, thought and values?'

Two aspects of self-reliance were commonly referred to by the Group of Leaders interviewed for this book. Firstly, it was acknowledged that strong leaders nearly always decide if something is right or wrong based on their own internal judgement. They go to an internal reference. This is not to say that they are unaware of or are ignoring other peoples' expectations and needs. Indeed those are listened to and assimilated into their decision-making process. However, effective leaders create and learn to depend on their own internal guidance system – often referred to as instinct.

The second aspect of self-reliance was the ability to self-critique without affecting self-assurance. In the interviews it was striking how many leaders told anecdotes that showed they regularly review the success of their actions with a critical eye. But, *crucially*, they do not let negative  results reduce their confidence in their own abilities or likelihood of success. They are able to self-critique but also self-validate.

This is a highly effective form of self-coaching which everyone can learn to use. It starts with you honestly assessing the effectiveness of your actions. The starting point is: *'Did I get the outcome I wanted?'* The most effective way to do that is to review your actions as if you were watching someone else or watching the movie with yourself in it. This allows you to be more detached and factual in your feedback

---

[8] Newman, N. (2008) *Emotional Capitalists*, Chichester, England: John Wiley and Sons Ltd.

to yourself. Then you can plan your next action from a relatively dissociated and dispassionate perspective – allowing you to maintain a resourceful and competent state of mind for thinking forward.

The key to this technique is always to critique at the behaviour level and not at the identity level. For example, 'Rosie's talk with the team today did not inspire them to take action like she intended, so she will need to come back to this in a different way at the next meeting' rather than 'Rosie got that all wrong today because she doesn't do these talks well.' As you will probably recognise, the same is true for feedback you give to other people. It's a matter of training your own internal critical voice to give you respectful, specific, quality feedback you can take action on next time.

Self-reliance

Leaders' messages

I am the best judge of whether or not I've done something well because I will know inside whether I cut corners and whether I can respect the course I took or not.

Pamela Taylor, Water UK

Trust your inner eye. That is the thing you visualise and see intuitively as right. When I get those flashes of insight I have certainly never regretted pursuing them.

Michael McNicholas, ESB International

Reflective time

One of the key changes needed in moving from manager to leader is to realise that you need to shift the balance of how you use your time to incorporate more reflection. Learning to 'let go' was a phrase that was regularly used to describe one of the hardest parts of leadership.

Letting go of the need to be 'doing', and accepting you can add value by 'thinking and being' is hard for many if not most people. One reason this can be difficult for leaders is that often the rewards and even the feedback they get can be indirect and much further down the line than has been their experience to date. Learning to get possibly bigger rewards in the longer term takes a level of patience and belief that requires good self-management.

Well used, reflective time lets you:

> stand back and take stock of the organisation or group as a whole in a way others are not in a position to do;

> widen your perspective on the bigger picture to see new or different angles and possibilities;

> renew your own internal vision and commitment, giving renewed energy;

> consider options away from a pressurised environment;

> get in tune with and be congruent with your own emotions

For more on the general benefits of good listening and reflective thinking see Nancy Kline's book *Time to Think*.[9]

It is important to find the best place or best process for you to create productive reflective time. Some people find the presence and interaction of others gives them both energy and creativity. This reflection time can be through:

> formal sessions, usually offsite, where the 'agenda' allows experimentation and reflection;

> informal dialogue with someone else, such as a coach, allowing thinking time and space;

> going to conferences or other knowledge-sharing events stimulating the mind to roam more freely;

> time on your own where you can conduct an inner dialogue with relative peace.

Whatever your way of reflecting, the key thing is to make space to go and do it – regularly. It is especially important to do so when considering whether to make significant change or responding to major external change.

[9] Kline, N. (1999) *Time to Think*, London: Ward Lock.

Reflective time

Leaders' messages

It's very lonely to be thinking of things and for others to be doing them!

Spiro Santoni, RBS

It is a constant challenge to balance taking time out to think, versus time actually finding out what is going on . . . Different things work for different people. The extraverted thinkers need to gather groups of people around them and brainstorm. The introverted thinkers need to go and walk by the beach.

Mark Dearnley, Cable & Wireless plc

Aligned with reflecting is the ability to take time away and look in from the outside. This is wider than reflecting from an internal perspective only.

Michael McNicholas, ESB International

Managing your energy

As leader there will be a lot of pressures on your energy and time. Ensuring you maintain your energy levels for both the short- and long-term demands is very important.

As Stephen Covey points out in *Seven Habits*, effective people take time to 'sharpen the saw'. For some, one of the best ways to renew their energy is to find an activity that is creative or allows reflective time. For others it is focusing 100% on activities that are apparently unrelated, allowing the mind and body to rebalance. For example, some people renew their internal energy through physical activity such as running or walking. Others use creative activities such as painting, gardening and practical DIY projects. What is clear from all the effective leaders is that they take control of this area of their lives and learn what techniques work for them.

Decisiveness

Decisiveness is the ability to take timely decisions and live with them. Your leadership will
generally be judged by the decisions you make
– or fail to make.

Being willing to make the tough decisions is
often said to be the leader's job. For some
people simply making decisions and living with
them can be difficult. Having the courage to take responsibility is a
big factor in decisiveness. This book is designed to help you make
consistently better decisions – big and small. As one leader told me,
'*Sometimes it's more important to make <u>a</u> decision than to make the
right one.*'

Effective leaders recognise that timing can be as important in a
decision as the actual decision itself. Hasty decisions can be costly
but so can procrastination. Reading the context well and understanding when conditions are opportune is a key area of judgement. The
ability to time a decision well will increase when you are clear in your
objectives and listening with care to your stakeholders. Greater self-
reliance will also increase your willingness to make decisions even
with less than perfect information.

Decisiveness

Leaders' messages

Having clarity is more important than having perfection. Having a perfect answer that keeps changing is more of a problem than having a good enough answer where there is clarity. Doing nothing might give you time to look at the absolute perfect answer but you may not have the opportunity any more.

Chris Floyd, Rolls-Royce plc

You are employed as leaders to make decisions . . . your job is to make decisions on imperfect information and stick with the consequences, amending, or doing whatever to adapt.

Major General Peter Williams

Don't be afraid to change your mind if the known facts change. Willingness to change your mind is a strength. The problem is when people have their mind made up by the last person they spoke to.

Ian Hay Davison, former Governor of the London School of Economics and Chairman Ruffer LLP

Continued learning and development

Underpinning all the conversations with the Group of Leaders was a mindset that they were still constantly learning and developing. This partly comes from their characteristic 'restless curiosity'. It also comes through their awareness that leadership is a dynamic role because the context changes. Even if they have significant leadership talents, everyone has to continue to develop their leadership abilities. This is even more so in complex organisations with many stakeholders across broad geographies.

Effective leaders recognise that their success comes in part from their openness to feedback and willingness to make changes to improve performance. In this way they model the behaviours they want to see in the successful groups and organisations they lead.

Continued learning and development

Leaders' messages

Good leaders are open to feedback themselves, they are quite open to hearing how it is for people that they work with, things they could do better.

Bob Mason, Hawkswood Resources Ltd

I think you have to constantly be prepared to question yourself, to challenge yourself and be prepared to develop and grow. If you are exhibiting this mindset, this behaviour, this attitude, the chances are that your organisations will pick up on it too. If not, at least you have the credibility to challenge others because you are prepared to do the same to yourself. How can you expect people to change and grow if you are stuck?

Josef Waltl, Shell International Petroleum Company Ltd

If you want to assess your level of self-management and self-reliance, here are some questions to ask yourself:

➤ *How well does the image of you that others appear to see and respond to reflect your own self-image (based on feedback you receive)?*

➤ *Do you get feedback about yourself you don't understand?*

➤ *Do you understand your own internal decision-making process(es) and their inherent strengths and weaknesses?*

➤ *Do you regularly review the outcomes you achieve versus those you plan for and what may have caused any differences to arise?*

➤ *How often do you make hasty or too slow decisions – or no decision?*

➤ *How regularly do you step outside your comfort zone to meet different people or interact in different events to broaden your perspective?*

➤ *How much real thinking time is scheduled in your diary?*

The key messages about personal enablers

....

1 Good self-management and self-renewal are personal disciplines needed for effective leadership.

2 It is vital to adopt processes that renew your energy and thinking – build it into your diary.

3 Stop doing and start taking time to listen, absorb and respond effectively to the feedback around you.

4 Decisiveness is about having the courage to take decisions in the right time-frame and sometimes with imperfect information or results!

Conclusions

These leadership principles form an essential platform on which effective leadership is built. Unlike the dilemmas covered in Chapters 2 to 6, they do not have a dynamic quality where you change your position on a continuum depending on the context and where you are in the process of achieving your goals.

 These principles are fixed foundations that leaders need to build and maintain for themselves.

The key benefit of building and using these principles is that you will find it easier and more straightforward to make good leadership decisions. They will enable you to create the best path forward for yourself and those you lead. Another important benefit is that you will be modelling for others many of the messages you want to communicate to build an effective organisation around you.

The next chapter looks at how these leadership principles interact with each other to guide you to making better leadership decisions. Chapter 9 shows how applying these principles helps you make consistently better day-to-day decisions around the five ways to be a better leader by knowing:

➤ who to be accessible to, when – and why;

➤ how best to connect and communicate with people;

- ➤ how to treat people in ways they respect;
- ➤ who to delegate to in a motivating way;
- ➤ when to make change and why.

Consistently better decisions in these areas will make you a consistently better leader.

Chapter **8**

The Inner Compass – How to navigate leadership success

- Highlights (p. 188)
- The Inner Compass at work (p. 188)
- Developing your Inner Compass to be a better leader (p. 192)

➤ Effective leaders create an Inner Compass to guide successful decision making. The compass has three elements: vision and passion, values and connection with people, and personal enablers to allow self-management and self-reliance. These are described in more detail in Chapter 7.

➤ For sustainable successful leadership, all three elements of the compass must be strong.

➤ A strong Inner Compass is the foundation for consistently better judgements.

➤ In this chapter you will find how the elements of the Inner Compass work together and learn to use a variety of tools and processes to facilitate development of this part of leadership capability.

The Inner Compass at work

Chapter 7 – The leadership jigsaw, highlights the principles that successful leaders use to guide their thinking and behaviours. These are grouped into three specific themes:

1 Vision, passion and ambition.

2 Values and connecting with people.

3 Personal enablers: self-management and self-renewal.

It is intriguing to ask: if these principles are all shared by successful leaders, how do they work to make them better leaders? When linked together as shown in the diagram opposite they form a powerful foundation for guiding your choices and decisions as a leader. They become your 'Inner Compass'.

When all elements of the Inner Compass are strong, decisions become easier because of the following reasons:

➤ You are clear about what you want to achieve and are motivated to make it happen.

The Inner Compass

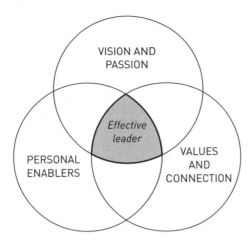

> You connect with and balance the needs of a range of people involved with or affected by your decisions – and engage them to come with you.

> You have created strong personal enablers to allow you to seek, listen and learn from feedback – giving you the energy, decisiveness and resilience to confidently meet challenges.

Developing a strong Inner Compass is invaluable whether you seek to simply lead your own self through life successfully or lead a team, a group or a whole organisation.

It is essential to develop all three elements for sustained effective leadership. If any one of the three elements is weak or missing, the imbalance limits your capacity to lead.

As shown in the diagram overleaf, if someone lacks the initial vision and passion, they struggle to be the leader themselves. They commonly find themselves in the role of a very good second-in-command to a more visionary leader. This is a role they can excel at as they combine the values and connection with people with the personal enablers. In this way they maintain energy and commitment to move the group forward and overcome challenges to deliver the desired results. They are natural Implementers.

People who are strong in the two elements vision and passion, and values and connection are good at creating desired futures other people can engage with and want to be part of. They are Ideas People.

Their leadership comes from creating a strong initial enthusiasm and following. However, if they lack the personal enablers they can be derailed. Low self-awareness can result in unchecked enthusiasm for a single way of doing things or make them unwilling to respond and learn from feedback. This leads to lopsided, patchy or poor results – or uncompleted initiatives. Lack of decisiveness can lead to ideas never getting off the ground. Sadly, for some people, when personal enthusiasm and commitment are not balanced with self-renewal, they can burn themselves out before they achieve their objectives.

Effect of missing elements in the Inner Compass

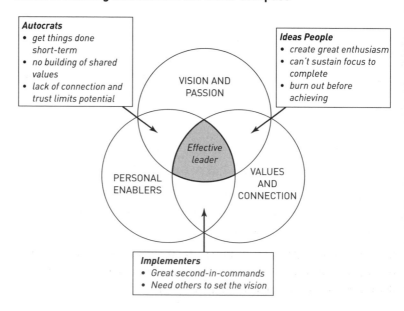

People who lack the values and cannot, or will not, connect with their followers develop into Autocrats. They are personally very clear about what they want to achieve and have strong self-assurance and will. They have personal enablers to allow them to renew their energy and they can build a team around them to complement individual strengths and weaknesses. Typically they are decisive and willing to take responsibility.

This style of leadership can be very effective over short timeframes and in periods of crisis and turnaround. But, over time, the Autocrat's lack of values and connection with their followers can create a sense of imposed rather than shared goals, imposed rather than shared values. People will wait to be told what to do rather than be inspired to take things forward for themselves. Communication will be top down only. The leader will be seen as distant and possibly feared rather than revered. The overall result will be significantly lower performance than the full potential of the group.

By now you may be asking, 'How do Implementers, Ideas People and Autocrats, relate to the Doormat Boss, Badger Boss and other characters found in Chapters 2–6?' The characters introduced in Chapters 2–6 describe what happens when a leader consistently uses one style of operation regardless of context. They become over-focused on one part of the leadership role. Some element of their Inner Compass is not as strong, reducing the effectiveness of their decision making.

For example, Doormat Bosses usually lack strong clarity about their vision and purpose but are strong on values and connecting with people. This imbalance then reduces the time they spend on reflection, renewing their energy and learning and developing. This in turn reduces their ability to step back, keep the bigger picture (the vision) in mind and prioritise accordingly. If left unchecked, Doormat Bosses may tend towards being an 'Implementer'. In contrast, the Badger Boss can see the bigger picture clearly and has strong vision and passion but is failing to connect with people and communicating all round. They may be strong in giving themselves reflective time but not so strong on seeking feedback and learning. If left unchecked they can become Autocrats.

If you diagnosed a tendency in yourself towards any of the 'Bosses' described in Chapters 2–6, the how-to sections in each chapter will help you reframe how you can make better decisions in response to the leadership dilemmas. Your ability to implement the how-to processes will be greatly enhanced if you also strengthen a part of your Inner Compass that is not strong enough.

So, if you have a tendency to act like a Doormat Boss, take time out to strengthen the vision, passion and ambition element of your Inner Compass. When you do, your ability to make good decisions about your time and accessibility will improve and you will transition towards being a Proactive Leader. Similarly, if you tend towards the Badger Boss, check how well you are connecting and being available to all your stakeholders over time. Are you fully respecting their needs and giving them the information they need to contribute fully?

It is tempting to try to put all of the 'boss' characters into some category within the Inner Compass model. This would be too broad a generalisation that does not necessarily reflect your needs as an individual reader. It is much more useful for you to review where you are stronger and weaker on the Inner Compass and understand how that feeds through into how and why you tend towards certain behaviour choices more than others. Balancing your decision-making processes by strengthening weaker elements of your Inner Compass will help you to be a better leader.

It is worth noting that being an 'effective leader' does not always mean someone is a 'good' leader in the moral sense. Sadly, there are some very effective but morally 'bad' leaders who cause untold harm. Like all effective leaders they connect with their followers and create shared values, but usually with very distorted and negative ways of expressing these values. Helping people develop the right moral values is outside the scope of this book.

Developing your Inner Compass to be a better leader

The principles that are presented in Chapter 7 and which make up the Inner Compass are the foundations for better leadership decisions in both your personal and professional life. Importantly, these elements are largely under your control. If you want to develop as a leader, a good place to start is to assess your own Inner Compass and refine and develop your capabilities in a structured way.

One way to assess your Inner Compass is to think of it in terms of a cockpit dashboard as shown in the diagram opposite.[1] The assessment may be your own self-assessment, in which case simply mark on the dials where you think you currently are. The absolute numbers are less important than getting the relative score for each piece of the Inner Compass.

Ideally get some additional data. Ask some people who work for and around you to give their assessment of your leadership capabilities (using a simple scale of 1, Low, to 10, High). Useful questions are:

[1] Copies of this worksheet are available from the website, **www.badgerordoormat.com**.

➤ *How clear is your vision as a leader?*

➤ *How strong is your passion and ambition for what the group or organisation does?*

➤ *How strongly do you model the values of respect, honesty and integrity?*

➤ *How connected are you with the people in the group or organisation and their shared values?*

➤ *How self-aware do they find you?*

➤ *How self-reliant?*

➤ *How often do you take reflective time to think?*

➤ *How well do you manage and renew your personal energy?*

➤ *How decisive are you?*

➤ *How well do you listen to feedback and learn?*

➤ *How well do you seek to learn and develop yourself?*

Inner Compass Dashboard

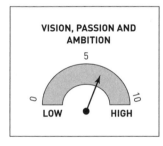

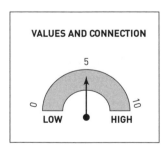

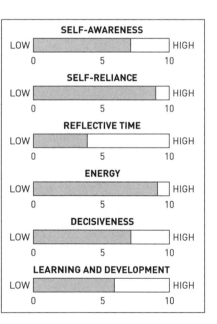

There are many ways to address further development including training programmes, on the job action learning activities, coaching and books.

When your Inner Compass is strong and balanced, each of the indicators on the dashboard will be pointing towards High. Where this is not the case, work on strengthening one or two elements at a time. You will have more success if you focus your development efforts.

Remember, the elements of the Inner Compass are the things where you have most control of and opportunity to develop your leadership capability. Take some time to consider what area of development will give you the most benefit in terms of strengthening your ability to make consistently good decisions. Create a development plan and look for live opportunities to practise, review and learn more.

Invest some time, effort and possibly some money in yourself. You wouldn't expect to walk into many jobs without some training, so why would you expect to do it as a leader?

Chapter **9**

Putting it all together – Ways to make better leadership decisions

- The big messages (p. 196)
- Handling leadership dilemmas (p. 196)
- Working across the dilemmas (p. 197)
- Outer decisions and the Inner Compass (p. 199)
- Developing your leadership skills (p. 202)

The big messages

Let's begin with the end in mind. The objective of this book is to provide practical ideas to enable you, the reader, to find ways to be a better leader. In the course of developing the materials and ideas for this book, including those from the Group of Leaders,[1] some big messages came out:

1 Leadership is a dynamic activity – it requires continual flexing across a range of dilemmas to deliver your chosen outcomes through other people.

2 It starts with creating clarity about the outcomes you and your group or organisation want.

3 Leadership effectiveness is increased by resolving certain key dilemmas effectively, using sound processes to develop your judgement.

4 Certain principles, values and habits will increase your capacity to make good decisions around the dilemmas – they form your Inner Compass to guide decision making.

This chapter explores these messages before looking at how to develop further and maintain your leadership abilities.

Handling leadership dilemmas

Chapters 2 to 6 looked at how to handle five common leadership dilemmas:

> best use of time – becoming a Proactive Leader;

> best way to communicate – becoming a Connecting Leader;

> how to treat people – becoming an Inspiring Leader;

> delegation and motivation – becoming a Coaching Leader;

> deciding when to make changes – becoming a Driving Leader.

One of the most important points about these dilemmas is they will always be with you. Handling them well is a part of the daily task of leadership.

[1] The Group of Leaders refers to the 20 successful leaders interviewed for this book whose biographies can be found at the back of the book.

The decisions you make in respect of these dilemmas strongly affect how you will be perceived as a leader – and how effective you will be. They are in effect the external micro levers you personally control to influence the outcomes your team or organisation achieve.

The second most important message is that leadership is a dynamic process. You need to regularly reassess and flex your choices of where to be on each dilemma continuum to match:

> ➤ the context you are in;

> ➤ the needs of the group you lead;

> ➤ the outcome(s) you are pursuing.

As all politicians and experienced leaders know, events will happen and require a change of priorities. Even without unpredictable events, conditions and contexts change. Hopefully, progress is made and results are delivered. Effective leaders are looking ahead, assessing today's and tomorrow's context and changing choice of behaviour appropriately.

Working across the dilemmas

As discussed in Chapter 1, the art of leadership is realising you can't be good at all aspects of it at the same time. Your focus and choice of response to the leadership dilemmas will vary over time.

Imagine you had a Dilemma Dashboard with a dial to show you where your focus was on each dilemma continuum at any given point in time. If, for example, you are just starting to decide whether to make a major change, the dials may look as shown on the first dashboard overleaf.

Your time will be focused on proactively talking to a fairly wide range of stakeholders while you gather information about the possibilities and implications of the change. Your communication will be focused more on expectation setting and listening rather than specific task-oriented conversations. Your people interaction will be less commanding but will not be entirely accommodating as you want to avoid setting up false expectations about what the change might mean.

In this mode your delegation style will be more towards blue sky as you invite a few people to think about designing the change and what may be possible. Finally, you may slightly reduce the number of other change initiatives being started so that, if you want to go ahead with the major change, you will not overload the system. Overall you will be in listening and preparation mode.

Dilemma Dashboard
Example: starting to decide on major change

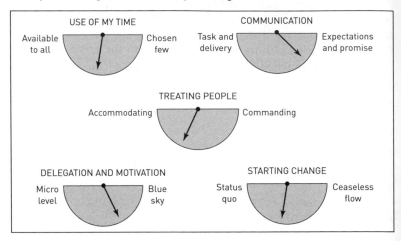

The Dilemma Dashboard will look very different at other times. For example, if you need to temporarily go into fire-fighting mode because a major customer has told you it is moving to a competitor, your Dilemma Dashboard may look like this:

Dilemma Dashboard
Example: short-term fire-fighting

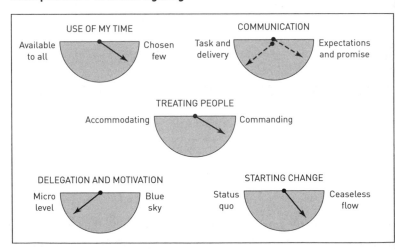

You will be focusing on a few key people in your own organisation and the customer's. Your communication will be alternating rapidly between listening and setting expectations externally and getting the task done internally. You are likely to be more commanding in style and delegating at a more micro level. You will be driving changes quickly in the organisation to try to match the customer's needs and retain their business. Overall you may be in 'short-term action' mode for a short period of time while you deal with the crisis to a point where you are confident someone else can handle it going forward.

You can use the concept of a Dilemma Dashboard to think through where your focus should be across the dials for different challenges. It is also a useful tool to analyse what needs to change if you regularly experience unsatisfactory results in one area of your leadership. In this situation, plot where your focus has been across the five dilemmas to see if you are overly focused or inappropriately focused in one area and out of alignment with what's needed overall.

Experienced leaders recognise when one aspect of their decision-making focus is misaligned with their decisions about the other dilemmas and learn to adjust accordingly.

Whether you are thinking through starting a major change or firefighting as discussed above, your Inner Compass should not be changing. Your vision, values and personal enablers are there to help you make good decisions under this added pressure.

Being able to choose the right behaviours is one part of the art of leadership. Being able to consistently perform those behaviours is another part. This is where the Inner Compass comes in.

Outer decisions and the Inner Compass

The decisions you make with respect to different leadership dilemma choices influence how the outside world experiences your leadership.

As shown in the diagram overleaf, the external decisions you make in response to the dilemmas are strongly interconnected with your Inner Compass (which is described in detail in Chapter 8). A strong Inner Compass helps a leader make better outer decisions about the dilemmas. It allows you to create drive, capacity and confidence.

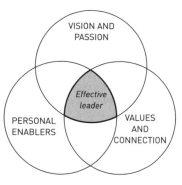

INNER COMPASS

How you create drive, capacity and confidence

EXTERNAL DECISIONS

How the world sees you and evaluates your effectiveness

TIME – THE PROACTIVE LEADER

∧

**COMMUNICATON –
THE CONNECTING LEADER**

∧

**PEOPLE INTERACTION –
THE INSPIRING LEADER**

∧

**DELEGATION AND MOTIVATION –
THE COACHING LEADER**

∧

CHANGE – THE DRIVING LEADER

∧

An effective Inner Compass increases your capacity to make good decisions

Learning from resolving dilemmas refines your Inner Compass

People who develop as better leaders create a positive feedback loop. They understand that as you learn to flex and improve your decisions with respect to the leadership dilemmas, so you learn how to develop and refine your Inner Compass effectively. Regular reviewing on how you make decisions and how successful they are gives you feedback about how clear your sense of direction is, how well people connect with your communications, how well you understand your stakeholders needs and so on. This creates a positive learning cycle leading to better leadership.

The ways in which two of the Inner Compass elements, vision, passion and ambition, and values and connection, help you to make better decisions with respect to the five leadership dilemmas is shown in the table opposite.

The third element, strong personal enablers, increases your ability to be a dynamic leader by allowing you to:

> step back and look at the wider picture;

> seek feedback and interaction to understand others;

> make timely decisions;

> stay resilient in the face of uncertainty, obstacles or set-backs;

> continually reflect, enquire and learn so you broaden your capabilities and avoid getting stuck in single mode;

> be a role model for others even under pressure or challenge.

How the Inner Compass creates better decisions about leadership dilemmas

Leadership dilemma	Inner Compass **VISION, PASSION AND AMBITION** Clear vision allows you to:	Inner Compass **VALUES AND CONNECTION** Strong expressed values, including respect, honesty and integrity, enable you to:
Time and accessibility	• prioritise who and what to focus your time on • decide how to shift that focus as things change	• give time and attention to things that matter to people as well as getting tasks done • be open about the focus of your time and subsequent availability
Communication	• engage with your stakeholders to create compelling goals • successfully communicate results and attainments in relationship to the group's 'cause'	• engage and connect with people in an open and transparent way • build trust in what you say and do
People interaction	• attract people who are engaged by that vision and purpose and wish to come with you • build a group 'cause' successfully	• treat people in ways they perceive as fair and appropriate • build trust in your leadership
Delegation and motivation	• understand what strengths, skills and resources will be needed to achieve the goals • align and motivate people to take responsibility through connection to purpose and vision	• understand what is expected of them and where they stand • give people opportunity and feedback that lets them develop and contribute fully
Starting change	• decide what priority changes are required to deliver the vision • set high standards and challenging goals	• give proper consideration of other stakeholders' needs when deciding upon change • explain the need for change in terms people understand

Developing your leadership skills

Can you develop and increase your capabilities to lead? This touches on the question: are great leaders born or can one learn the craft?

My answer is 'Both'. As one of the Group of Leaders put it, '**No one was born an executive director – everyone has things to learn.**'

Clearly some people have more natural talent in the basic elements of leadership. If that talent is combined with an early interest in taking leadership roles, then they are likely to put themselves forward for those roles at a younger age and so create opportunities to learn and hone their skills. As Malcolm Gladwell points out in his book *Outliers*,[2] highly successful people in any field of life are often the product of:

> early selection based on some early expressed talent; and

> a great deal of practice.

There are also people with the potential and capacity to lead, albeit at different levels of complexity and in different contexts, who only get the interest or opportunity at a later point in life. Given sufficient opportunity and development feedback, there is nothing to stop them significantly expanding their leadership capability.

For some that opportunity may come about by quirks of fate – they suddenly find themselves in a situation where their style matches the needs of the group and context and they fit the role of leader. Others may seek out leadership development in a more conscious and organised way.

Interestingly, the two military leaders in the Group of Leaders talked about a system of development where everyone is given the leadership training appropriate to their level. Some will respond well, learn, implement the lessons and be promoted to lead more complex challenges. They will then be given further development training appropriate to that level and so on. Those that don't learn or develop the skills will stay at the same level. The military leaders in the Group of Leaders planned on around 10% of their senior people's time to be spent on leadership development courses and

[2] Gladwell, M. (2008) *Outliers*, London: Penguin Books Ltd.

initiatives. Hence the leadership capacity of their whole group is being constantly increased and renewed.

Systematic leadership development like this is much rarer in the commercial world but can be found in some, usually larger, organisations. Increasingly, it is up to individuals to take control of their own development and look for, and create, development opportunities formally and informally in their lives.

So my answer is yes, definitely you can develop your leadership capabilities if you want to. The fact that you are reading this book already indicates your interest.

For most people in leadership roles, better leadership is achieved by making consistently better decisions on a daily basis about the types of dilemmas covered in this book. When you strengthen the elements of your Inner Compass, such as increasing your clarity of vision, you are upgrading your thinking and mindset. This translates into more successful decisions on a range of issues. This is how leadership development translates into leadership success.

When you are a better leader it improves not only your own success but also that of many people round you. Better leadership leads to:

➤ achieving your group or organisation's outcomes with more ease;

➤ your team knowing where they are going and feeling inspired to meet the challenge;

➤ your organisation developing more capable and effective people who find their jobs more satisfying;

➤ your customers getting better products and services;

➤ your financial backers and/or shareholders having confidence in your organisation;

➤ your own days being more productive and satisfying as you can work faster, be more 'user-friendly' and handle complexity with more ease.

When you master the art of resolving dilemmas well, you become a Proactive, Connecting and Inspiring Leader. You understand how to be a Coaching Leader for people and a Driving Leader for your organisation. Your stakeholders will see and feel the difference, allowing your whole group or organisation to lift its performance and achieve its ambitions.

So I invite you to implement your learning from this book. Continue to look, listen and learn – but most of all enjoy being an effective leader.

Biographies of the Leaders

The biographies of the Group of Leaders are written to reflect their role and company position at the time they were interviewed for this book. In the subsequent period between the interview and the time of publication, some leaders may have moved to new roles which are not reflected here.

Major-General John Chester, OBE, BA (Hons)

Formerly chief executive of the Chartered Institute of Management Accountants (CIMA), a body that offers an internationally-recognised professional qualification in management accountancy, John was commissioned into the Royal Marines in 1963 after studying at St Joseph's College, Ipswich, and served until 1995. Twice mentioned in dispatches, he served in Borneo, Norway, Ulster and the Falklands campaign for which he was awarded an OBE. From 1989–91 he was chief of staff at Special Forces HQ, followed by spells as brigadier commanding the Marines Training and Reserve Forces and on the staff of the RCDS. He has also been a governor of the Royal Naval Scholarship Fund, is a lay member of the Special Immigration Appeals Commission, has sat on the Hampshire CC Standards Committee, and recently completed a full-time Fine Arts degree.

Mike Clare

Mike Clare is founding owner and chief executive of Dreams, Britain's leading bed specialist. It comprises over 170 bed superstores nationwide and has its own UK manufacturing facility capable of producing over one million beds a year. Since 1987, when he opened his first bed shop in Uxbridge, the company has grown until its turnover in 2007 approached £200m. Dreams's growth has broken records year on year and the company now employs over 1500 people.

Mike is also a non-executive director of the British Retail Consortium, president of the Furnishing Trades Benevolent Association, an ambassador for Buckinghamshire and a Freeman of the City of London, as well as a patron of The Outward Bound Trust.

Mark Dearnley

Mark Dearnley is chief information officer at Cable & Wireless International responsible for the IT functions across the business. Cable & Wireless is one of the world's leading international communications companies. The International business unit operates integrated telecommunications companies in 33 countries, with principal operations in the Caribbean, Panama, Macau, Monaco and the Channel Islands.

Mark joined Cable & Wireless through its acquisition of Energis. Before that he was chief operating officer at Boots.com where he also held a number of senior IT management positions. Previously, he worked as a management consultant, and in manufacturing management in the aerospace industry. He holds a degree in Electrical and Electronic Engineering, is a Fellow of the IEE and a chartered engineer.

Chris Floyd

Dr Chris Floyd is business development director for Rolls-Royce plc, responsible for developing the strategies for growing the company's non-aerospace businesses, which include marine, energy, and technology-based enterprises.

Rolls-Royce is a global power systems company providing power for land, sea and air, with leading positions in civil aerospace, defence, marine and energy markets. Its customer base includes airlines, armed forces, including 70 navies, and energy and marine customers in 120 countries. Rolls-Royce employs over 39,000 people in over 50 countries. Annual sales in 2007 were £7.4 bn, with the non-aerospace businesses accounting for £2.1bn of this.

Previously Chris was a European director for Arthur D Little, the management and technology consultancy, and has worked for the past 25 years on growth strategies for technology-based products companies, in the aerospace, engineering, electronics, medical and consumer goods industries. He was educated at Cambridge and Bristol Universities and London Business School, and has a degree in Engineering, a PhD in Aeronautical Engineering, and an MBA. Chris Floyd is the author of *Managing Technology for Corporate Success.*

Catherine Gronquist

At the time of the interview, Catherine Gronquist was associate director of research at Morgan Stanley. She spent nearly 27 years at Morgan Stanley, mostly in institutional sales, where she covered the Nordic countries, Benelux and latterly, the UK. She was made director of international fixed income research in mid-2005 and joined the management team of the integrated research team at Morgan Stanley in January 2006. Her previous experience includes positions at Salomon Brothers, USWest and Union Pacific Railroad. Until November 2007, when it was sold to Mark-It Partners, she represented Morgan Stanley on the board of International Index Company, a multi-contributor index consortium.

Catherine is the senior sponsor of the London Women's Network, WFC, a Morgan Stanley initiative and represents the firm on the board of The Competitor Diversity Forum, an organisation that examines ways to expand the number of women entering the investment banking arena.

Catherine graduated from the University of Denver in 1977 with a Bachelor of Arts and received a Masters of Business Administration in 1978.

Ian Hay Davison, CBE

Ian Hay Davison was chairman of the Regulatory Council of the Dubai International Financial Centre and a governor of the London School of Economics. Ian joined the London office of Arthur Andersen & Co in 1958 as their first 'computer expert', rising to managing partner in 1966. Under his management, staff numbers grew from 180 to 2000. His career as a financial watchdog began when he was appointed as the DTI inspector in the Stonehouse case in 1975. Ian joined Lloyd's in 1983 and as the first outside chief executive of the then self-regulating Lloyd's of London, Ian is credited as the man who cleaned up Lloyd's, unearthing many malpractices and introducing new rules.

He has also filled, among other roles, chairman of Credit Lyonnais Capital Markets, Storehouse plc, Northgate plc, and The NMB plc (a Bank of England subsidiary); director of Newspaper Publishing plc (*The Independent*), and of the Royal Opera House. Ian has a BSc in Economics from the LSE, and also attended the University of Michigan.

Michael McNicholas

Michael McNicholas is executive director of ESB International (ESBI), the major commercial subsidiary of ESB, Ireland's largest power company. ESB is Ireland's premier utility and is the owner, developer and operator of 5000 MW of generating capacity in Ireland. ESBI builds, owns and operates power stations, as well as providing a full range of engineering and consultancy services to clients worldwide. With over 1000 staff, ESBI's expertise covers all aspects of energy projects, from concept to development to operation and maintenance. To date ESBI has carried out projects in over 115 countries.

Michael has 25 years' experience in the power industry and 12 years in senior leadership positions. He has experience in both large customer-facing businesses in electricity retail and network services and also the heavy production environment of power generation. He also led a major change programme across ESB Group designed to meet the challenges driven by deregulation and the introduction of competition to the Irish electricity market.

Bob Mason

After a long career with BT where he was HR director for BT's UK business, Bob now works as an interim HR executive, consultant and executive coach. Recent corporate roles have included: HR director for Wolseley UK, the UK operating company of Wolseley plc, the world's number one distributor of heating and plumbing products and a leading supplier of builders' products to the professional market. Prior to joining Wolseley, Bob worked as a strategic HR adviser in the Department of Health. He was also interim HR director at London Underground in the run-up to the conclusion of the Public Private Partnership which secured massive investment for the Tube network.

For six years he was non-executive deputy chairman of the Employers' Forum on Disability. He was also chairman of the Equal Pay Task Force, set up by the Equal Opportunities Commission to review the UK's Gender Pay Gap. He is a graduate of the Universities of Lancaster (BSc in Management Science/Operational Research) and Liverpool (MBA), and is a Chartered Fellow of the Chartered Institute of Personnel and Development.

Roger Mountford

Following a career as a merchant banker in London and Hong Kong, Roger Mountford now serves on a number of boards in the public and private sectors. He is chairman of The Housing Finance Corporation and HgCapital Trust plc, a governor of the London School of Economics and Political Science (LSE) and chairman of its commercial subsidiary Enterprise LSE Ltd. He is appointed by the Secretary of State for Transport as a board member of the Civil Aviation Authority (CAA) and deputy chairman of the Port of Dover.

The Housing Finance Corporation (THFC) is an independent, specialist, finance company that issues long-term funds and borrows from the European Investment Bank, in order to on-lend to Registered Social Landlords for the construction of social housing and regeneration projects across the United Kingdom. HgCapital Trust is an award-winning listed investment trust specialising in leveraged buyouts in the UK and northern Europe. The LSE is the world's leading university specialising in the social sciences; through Enterprise LSE the School's academics provide consultancy services and executive education programmes to clients in many countries.

The CAA is the UK's specialist aviation regulator. Its activities include economic regulation, airspace policy, safety regulation and consumer protection. The Port of Dover is one of the world's busiest ro-ro ports and the UK's second largest cruise port.

Roger was educated at the LSE and Stanford Business School.

Dave Mutton

Dave Mutton is an electrical engineer and IT professional with over 25 years' experience at senior executive level in the electricity industry. Chief executive of ElectraLink Ltd, which provides vital data transfer services to the UK's electricity market, he led the company through the re-procurement of the DTS and the transition to the new service from EDS. ElectraLink Ltd was established to create a fast, reliable and secure electronic means of communicating data between participants in the competitive electricity market, and has established a reputation for service excellence in transferring business-critical data in a secure, reliable and cost-effective way. Dave has also developed a commercial income stream for ElectraLink by providing secretarial and administrative support services to DCUSA Ltd in the electricity market, and to SPAA Ltd in the gas market, and commercial data transfer and processing services to both industries.

Prior to this, Dave was chief executive of St Clements Services Ltd, which he joined after a long career as a director of SWEB, helping to change the culture of the company after privatisation. He also spent time at Yorkshire, Midlands, Norweb and Eastern Electricity.

Dorothy Nesbit

Dorothy is an executive coach (Learning for Life (Consulting) Ltd) with 20 years' experience in developing leadership at individual and organisational level through leadership research, executive assessment, leadership development and 1:1 coaching. Dorothy works with high-potential leaders, from first-time leaders through to established directors and CEOs. Dorothy has consulted widely across sectors in the UK, Europe and beyond, including the finance, insurance, pharmaceutical, professional and education sectors.

Whilst Dorothy's work is mainly in the private sector, she has a special interest in leadership in schools. She has been a voluntary judge for the Teaching Awards since 2003 and is currently chair of the South Eastern Regional Judging Panel and a member of the National Judging Team for the category of The Royal Air Force Award for Headteacher of the Year in a Secondary School. She is also Entrepreneur in Residence at the Federation of Chalvedon School and Sixth Form College and Barstable School. She is also co-founder of School Coach, a fledgling organisation which brings coaches into schools on a voluntary basis to support the development of leadership in schools.

Dorothy began coaching early in her career, both as a coach to leaders participating in leadership development programmes and as a coach and mentor to professional colleagues. In 2004 she completed a professional coach training certified by the International Coaching Federation and now places executive coaching at the centre of her work. Dorothy has an MA (Cantab), is a certified NLP Coach and member of the International Coach Federation and a fellow of the Royal Society of Arts.

Spiro Santoni

Spiro Santoni is head of active credit portfolio management at RBS Global Banking & Markets, which provides a range of debt financing, risk management and investment services to leading corporations and financial institutions.

Previously with The Royal Bank of Scotland, Spiro fulfilled a number of roles including being appointed sole head of risk for financial markets, a role he had previously filled at Yamaichi International (Europe). Before this, after working in Paris, London and Norway as a senior naval architect, Spiro joined LIFFE in product development.

He studied Naval Architecture and Ocean Dynamics at Glasgow University, completing a BSc and a PhD, and later went on to achieve an MBA in Finance at City University Business School.

John Shine

John Shine is managing director of ESB Networks, the transmission and distribution arm of ESB, Ireland's largest power company. ESB Networks builds, operates and maintains the Irish electricity distribution system and it also owns and constructs the national transmission system. ESB Networks has invested over €5 billion in renewing, reinforcing and extending Ireland's electricity infrastructure since the start of this decade.

Before leading ESB Networks, John held a number of senior positions in the networks, marketing and business development areas of the company. He also spent some years outside ESB developing a successful international services business before rejoining in 2002. He was educated at University College Dublin and has a degree in Electrical Engineering and an MBA.

Chong-Meng Tan

Chong-Meng Tan is executive vice president of Global Business-to-Business (B2B) for Shell, headquartered in London and Singapore. He manages six global lines of businesses that sell fuels and speciality products to commercial customers, namely Aviation, Marine, Commercial Fuels, Bitumen, LPG and Sulphur. The business spans 80 countries with about 5000 staff handling a total sales volume of about 2 million barrels per day.

He is a member of the Shell Downstream Management team, a director on Showa Shell Board in Japan and serves as regional business director, overseeing the alignment among the global downstream business interests in the Asia Pacific countries where Shell operates. His long international career in Shell includes positions in retail, marketing, strategy, international trading, and refining. Besides Shell he also serves as a director on the board of Fraser and Neave Ltd, a property-cum-food and beverage company listed in Singapore. Before joining Shell, he worked with the Government of Singapore in the Ministry of National Development in various capacities.

Chong-Meng Tan is a Malaysian and he graduated from the National University of Singapore in 1983 and holds Bachelor and Master's degrees in Mechanical Engineering and Industrial Engineering respectively. He also completed a senior executive programme at the University of Columbia in 2003.

Pamela Taylor, OBE

Pamela Taylor is a founder director and the first chief executive of Water UK and was previously chief executive of the Water Companies Association before winding it up to form Water UK. Water UK is the industry association which represents the UK's statutory water supply and waste water companies at national and European level. It is funded by its members to influence public policy and opinion to ensure a strong water industry in the interests of all stakeholders. Its core objective is sustainable water policy to create lasting benefit by integrating economic, environmental and social objectives.

Pamela is a former president of both the European Union of National Associations of Water Suppliers and Waste Water Services and the Chartered Institute of Public Relations.

She was the BBC's director of corporate affairs worldwide and before that she headed up the British Medical Association's public policy. She has worked as a management consultant for the World Health Organisation, the NHS and the Design Council. Her charity work includes being treasurer and trustee for the Royal Society of Arts, a trustee of WaterAid and the Royal Society for Public Health, a patron of the Institute of Water Officers and being involved with the Foundation for AIDS, and Children in Need.

Pamela is also a mentor to senior business leaders with the London First Scheme.

David Vaughan

David Vaughan is a partner and head of the corporate group at Wragge & Co LLP, a top-25 UK law firm. Apart from a reputation of technical and service excellence, Wragge & Co invests strongly in its people and is the only law firm to appear in both the *Sunday Times* 100 Best Companies To Work For and the *Financial Times* 50 Best Workplaces in the UK. As head of corporate, David leads a team of 17 equity partners and 70 lawyers and is responsible for revenues of £20m. This means something of a multi-faceted existence – part leader, part manager and part transactional lawyer advising on mergers and acquisitions.

Josef Waltl

Josef Waltl is executive vice-president, retail for Shell International Petroleum Company Limited, Shell's global Retail business. Operating 45,000 petrol retailing sites in 90 countries around the world, the company serves over 20 million customers every day. Over one million people work on the business through dealerships, partnerships and related activities. Josef is Austrian and has a 30-year career with Shell.

Major General Peter Williams, CMG, OBE

Currently a defence consultant, lecturer and battlefield tour guide, Peter Williams was commissioned into the Coldstream Guards in 1972 after studying history at Cambridge and served as an infantry officer in Berlin, Ulster, Oman, Hong Kong, Germany and Bosnia, as well as the Gambia, Kenya, Brunei and Canada. He was regimental intelligence officer for three years and, as a qualified Russian interpreter, spent over four years in liaison and intelligence duties in East Germany, for which he was awarded an MBE.

Following two years as UK military assistant/speechwriter to the Supreme Allied Commander Europe, he commanded the 1st Battalion Coldstream Guards in East Tyrone and as part of the peacekeeping force during the war in central Bosnia (OBE), later returning (as a colonel) as deputy chief of the UN Peace Force Military Observer group and subsequently working in Whitehall as the assistant director intelligence responsible for overseeing the Yugoslav crisis. Following this, as a brigadier, he was the chief liaison officer in NATO HQ in Sarajevo.

He later served in Brussels as the deputy UK military representative to the European Union, and then, as a major general, was the first head of the NATO Military Liaison Mission in Moscow, for which he received a CMG. After leaving the army in 2005 Peter spent a sabbatical year as a lecturer at Australasian Defence Force academies lecturing on NATO, the EU, Russia, operations and military ethics.

John Wybrew

After eight years as executive director of British Gas and its successor companies, John Wybrew retired from the board of National Grid Transco, the company which provides gas and electricity infrastructure. He is now chairman of the Sector Skills Council, which tackles the skills needs of the gas, electricity, water and waste management industries; of the British Energy Association and the Foundation for Management Education; and of two commercial enterprises. He also sits on the board of the Energy Regulator, Ofgem, and of Henley Management College.

Before joining the board of British Gas in 1996, John had a wide-ranging 30-year career in the international oil and gas industry with the Shell Group, ending up on the board of Shell UK. For three years in the mid-1980s, he was seconded to the Prime Minister's Policy Unit as the adviser for energy and transport.

Index

Page numbers in *italics* denotes an illustration/table

abilities, unique 111, 112
accessibility 11–36
  acknowledging own needs and
    preferences 31
  and Badger Boss 12, 13, 15–16,
    18–19, 22, 26, 29, 31, 191
  Badger Boss diagnostic 17
  and Doormat Boss 12, 13–15,
    14, 18, 22, 23, 26, 29, 30, 31,
    191
  Doormat Boss diagnostic 16–17
  and Inner Compass *201*
  and planning of time *see* time,
    planning of
  and prioritising 21–4
  and Proactive Leader 12, 19–31,
    196
  Proactive Leader in action 32–3
  and voting wisely 30–1
accountability, managing 119, 166
acknowledgement, of people's
    capabilities 115, 116, 123
Adams, Douglas 52
ambition 163–8, 188, 200
appraisal
  of current situation and
    performance 139
Ashley, Mike 53
audio conferencing 26
Autocrats 190–1
automated meeting request
    systems 25

Badger Boss 12, 13, 15–16, 18–19,
  22, 26, 29, 31, 191

  diagnostic 17
Barking Boss 99–101, *101*, 106–7
  diagnostic 104
behaviours
  setting and maintaining 80–4,
    93
'Blunt Truth' style 54–6, *54*
Bohn, Roger 30
bonding 53–4, 66
Branson, Richard 53

Cairo, P. 88
capabilities
  acknowledging 115, 116, 123
  matching to tasks 111–13
cause
  creating and communicating the
    76–80
change 127–60, 179
  assessing capability for 148–53,
    158
  assessing need to 138–43
  assessing what to 143–4
  assessing when to 153–5
  commitment to 152
  considering benefits and costs
    of 144–8, 157
  denial and resistance to 152,
    153
  and Dilemma Dashboard 197–8,
    198
  and DREC model 151–3
  and Driving Leader 136–55, 196
  Driving Leader in action 155–7
  and Inner Compass *201*

change (*continued*)
  key levers for and linking of
    143, *144*, 157
  and productivity cycle 135–6, *135*
  and Runaway Boss 130, 131–3,
    132, 136, 145–6, 148, 150, 155
  Runaway Boss diagnostic 134
  and Tortoise Boss 130–1, *131*,
    136, 141–2, 145, 148, 150–1,
    155
  and Tortoise Boss diagnostic
    133–4
Chester, Major General John 171,
  205
choices, making good 2
Clare, Mike 166, 205–6
coaching approach 116–17, 122
Coaching Leader 107–15, 120–1,
  196
Collins, J. and Porras, J.
  Built to Last 164
Collins, Jim 167
  Good to Great 59, 111, 162
comfort zone 113
commitment, and change 152
communication 37–64, 167
  assigning credit and blame 59,
    62
  balancing between managing
    the message and managing
    the results 45–8
  'Blunt Truth' versus 'Good Story'
    style 54–7, *54*, *56*
  and bonding 53–4
  choosing style to fit the situation
    56–7, 62
  and Connecting Leader 48–59,
    196
  Connecting Leader in action
    59–61
  connecting with people's needs
    and motivations 47
  creation of 'listening' channels
    52
  and Empty Trumpeter 39, 42–3,
    43, 46–7, *46*, 51
  and Empty Trumpeter
    diagnostic 44–5

flexibility in 53–9
  and Inner Compass *201*
  knowing when to communicate
    51–3
  leader's role in connecting with
    stakeholders 22, 46, 48, *48*
  managing stakeholders 49–51,
    62
  and Misunderstood Martyr 39,
    40–1, *41*, 46, *46*, 51
  Misunderstood Martyr
    diagnostic 44
  and outcome-setting 110
  self-awareness of your own
    preferred style of 58, 62
  as vital leadership skill 58
  ways of reinforcing positive
    messages 52
Connecting Leader 48–59, 59–61,
  196
connecting with people
  and values 168–74, 189, 190
  See also interaction
continued learning and
  development 175, 182–4
Corporate Leadership Council
  115
cost/benefit analysis 145–6
Covey, Stephen
  Habits of Highly Effective People
    163, 180
credit, assigning of 59, 62
culture, organisation's 80–2, 118
  and feedback 118
  group-level negotiables
    segment 81, 82
  individual-level negotiables
    segment 82, 83
  non-negotiable segment 81, 82,
    92, 93
curiosity 66, 85–7, 93, 117
  restless 140, 182

Dearnley, Mark 169, 173, 180, 206
decisions
  and decisiveness 175, 181–2,
    184, 190
  ways to make better 195–204

decisiveness 175, 181–2, 184, 190
delegation 20, 28, 97–125
  acknowledging of people's
      capabilities 115, 116, 123
  and Barking Boss 99–101, *101*,
      106–7
  Barking Boss diagnostic 104
  and being fair 114–15
  and Coaching Leader 107–15,
      196
  Coaching Leader in action 120–
      1
  dealing with poor performance
      119
  getting and giving feedback
      115–19
  and Inner Compass *201*
  managing accountability 119,
      123
  matching right people to the
      task 105, 111–13, 122
  outcome-setting 108–10, 122
  playing to people's strengths
      114
  and Superhero Boss 99, 102–3,
      103, 107
  Superhero diagnostic 104–5
  and training 113, 122
  using diversity to drive
      performance 113–15, 122
Denning, Stephen
  *The Secret Language of
      Leadership* 57–8
diaries 25
Dilemma Dashboard 197–9, *198*
dilemmas, leadership 2–3, 196–
      201
  handling 196–7
  and Inner Compass 199–201,
      200, *201*
  working across 177–9
  See also accessibility; change;
      communication; delegation;
      interaction
Dilts, Robert 165
diversity
  using of to drive performance
      113–15, 122

Doom-monger 55
Doormat Boss 12, 13–15, *14*, 18,
      22, 23, 26, 29, 30, 31, 191
  diagnostic 16–17
Dotlich, D.L. *et al*
  Head, Heart and Guts 88
DREC (Denial, Resistance,
      Exploration, Commitment)
      change model 151–3, *151*
Driving Leader 136–55, 155–7,
      196

'ego-free listening' 140
'elevator' speech 28
Emperor Boss 66, 69–71, *70*, 72–
      3, 78–9, 83–4, 87
  diagnostic 72
Empty Trumpeter 39, 42–3, *43*,
      46–7, *46*, 51
  diagnostic 44–5
energy, managing your 175, 180–
      1
expectations
  setting and maintaining 80–4

fair, being
  and delegation 114–15
feedback 157, 162, 178, 183
  and coaching approach 116–17
  and culture 118, 123
  and delegation 123
  getting accurate and timely
      116–18
  as performance enhancer 115
feedback loop 87, 139, 199–200
fire-fighting syndrome 29–30
  and Dilemma Dashboard 198–9,
      198
flexibility 65–95
  in communication 53–9
Floyd, Chris 169, 182, 206–7
Franks, David 54
'Gandhi' test 49, 50
Gladwell, Malcolm
  Outliers 202
goal-setting 109, 110
'Good Story' style 54–6, *54*
Gossip 55

grapevine 52
greeting 73
Grinder, Michael 87–8
Gronquist, Catherine 173, 207
group cause 77–80, 93, 143
group dynamics 87–8
group-level negotiables 81, 82
groups
 balancing needs of against
  needs of individual 87–90,
  93
 reading needs of 84–7, 93

Hay, Ian Davison 207–8
Hippie Boss 66, 68–9, 69, 72–3,
 78, 83, 87, 89
 diagnostic 71
honesty 169, 171–2, 173–4

Ideas People 189
Implementers 189, 191
individual-level negotiables 82, 83
individuals
 balancing group needs with
  needs of 87–90, 93
 reading of 84–7, 93
Inner Compass 7, 29, 187–94, 189,
 196, 203
 assessing and developing of
  192–4, 193
 effect of missing elements in
  189–91, 190
 elements of 188–9, 189
 and leadership dilemmas 199–
  201, 200, 201
 and outer decisions 199–201
Inspiring Leader 74–90, 91–2, 196
instinct 177
integrity 169, 171–2, 173–4
interaction 65–95
 balancing of group and
  individual needs 73–4, 87–
  90
 creating and communicating the
  purpose and vision 76–80
 and Emperor Boss 66, 69–71,
  70, 72– 3, 78–9, 83, 87
 Emperor Boss diagnostic 72

and Hippie Boss 66, 68–9, 69,
 72–3, 78, 83, 87, 89
Hippie Boss diagnostic 71
and Inner Compass 201
and Inspiring Leader 74–90,
 91–2, 196
Inspiring Leader in action 91–2
reading individuals and groups
 84–7, 93
setting and maintaining values,
 behaviours and
 expectations 80–4
investor's strategy 165

Kline, Nancy
 Time to Think 179
Kohlrieser, Professor George 53–
 4
 Hostage at the Table 163
Kotter, John 149
 and Cohen, D.S.
  The Heart of Change 129

Latitude Consulting 76
leader, definition 3
leadership
 benefits of effective 203
 difference between
  management and 4
leadership skills,
 developing 202–4
leadership style 162, 163, 176
leadership talents 202
'let go', learning to 178–9
listening, ego–free 140
'listening channels', creation of
 52
London Wasps Rugby Club 118–
 19

McKinsey & Company 148
McNicholas, Michael 166, 178, 180,
 208
management
 difference between leadership
  and 4
manager, definition 3
Mason, Bob 183, 208–9

meeting technologies 26
meetings 29
messages
  clarity of 28
  ways of reinforcing positive 52
mind–mapping 49
mind's eye 163
mindsets, changing of 4–5
mission 165
Misunderstood Martyr 39, 40–1,
    41, 46, 46, 51
  diagnostic 44
moral values 192
motivation(s)
  acknowledgement as vital
    ingredient of 115
  connecting with people's 47
Mountford, Roger 170, 209
Mutton, Dave 165, 210

Nesbit, Dorothy 166, 210–11
Newman, Martyn
  Emotional Capitalists 103, 177
non–negotiables 81, 82, 92, 93

Obeng, Professor Eddie 75, 144
outcomes
  creating clarity of 196
  distinction from output 109
  setting of when delegating
    108–10, 119
outputs 109, *109*

PA/secretary, working with 24, 27
passion 163–8, 188, 200
people interaction *see* interaction
perceptions 73
performance
  feedback and enhancement of
    115
  using diversity to drive 113–15,
    122
performance reviews 118
permission to lead, building of 75,
    88, 93
personal enablers 174–84, 188,
    189, 200

continued learning and
    development 175, 182–4
decisiveness 175, 181–2, 184,
    190
managing your energy 175,
    180–1
reflective time 175, 178–80
self-awareness 175–6, 190
self-reliance 175, 177–8, 181
planning of time *see* time,
    planning of
poor performance, dealing with
    119
praise 116
presuppositions 84–5
prioritising 21–4
Proactive Leader 12, 19–31, 32–3,
    196
productivity cycle 135–6, *135*
purpose
  creating and communicating
    76–80

reading individuals and groups
    84–7, 93
reflective time 175, 178–80
requests
  filtering and dealing with 24–6
respect 73, 93, 169, 170, 173–4
review processes 118
Rhinesmith, S.H. 88
Roddick, Anita 53
rumour 55
Runaway Boss 130, 131–3, *132,*
    136, 145–6, 148, 150, 155
  diagnostic 134

Santoni, Spiro 171, 180, 211
scenario planning techniques 141
self–awareness 137, 162, 175–6,
    190
  of own communication style 58,
    62
self-confidence 176
self-critique 177–8
self-management
  and personal enablers 174–84,
    188

self-reliance 175, 177–8, 181
self-renewal 188
Seligman, Martin 111
shareholders 165
Shine, John 166, 211
signature strengths model 111–12
stakeholder mapping 49–51, *50*, 148
stakeholders
  and change 99, 104–5, 148
  leader's role in connecting with 22, 46, 48, *48*
  managing 49–51, 62
  reviewing possible impact of goals on key 110
STaRS model 149
strategic change 23
strategic priorities 21
strengths
  acknowledging of 115, 116, 122
signature 111–12
Sullivan, Dan 26, 111, 112
Superhero Boss 99, 102–3, *103*, 107
  diagnostic 104–5

Tan, Chong–Meng 169, 176, 212
tasks 109
Taylor, Pamela 171, 178, 212–13
team balance 137, 168–9
Time Burglars 14, 18
time planner *27*
time, planning of 18, 24–30
  dealing with and filtering of requests 24–6
  and delegation 28
  and fire-fighting syndrome 29–30

principles of good time organisation 26–9
using meeting technologies 26
working with secretary/PA 24, 27
Tortoise Boss 130–1, *131*, 136, 141–2, 145, 148, 150–1, 155
  diagnostic 133–4
training
  and delegation 113, 122
trust 172–4

under-promise and over-deliver rule 51
unique abilities model 111, 112

values
  and connecting with people 168–74, 169, 188, 200
  setting and maintaining 80–4
van der Heijden, Kees van *Scenarios* 141
Vaughan, David 166, 181, 213
video conferencing 26
vision
  creating and communicating 76–80, 163–8, 188, 189, 200
voting 30–1

Waltl, Josef 171, 176, 183, 213
Watkins, Michael 149
web meetings 26
Williams, Major General Peter 182, 213–14
Wybrew, John 173, 181, 214

BC	03/10

FAST TRACK TO SUCCESS

9780273719908

9780273721789

9780273721802

9780273719885

9780273719922

9780273721765

EVERYTHING YOU NEED TO ACCELERATE YOUR CAREER